THE HUGUENOT • EDWARD MERYON

Publisher's Note

The book descriptions we ask booksellers to display prominently warn that this is an historic book with numerous typos or missing text; it is not indexed or illustrated.

The book was created using optical character recognition software. The software is 99 percent accurate if the book is in good condition. However, we do understand that even one percent can be an annoying number of typos! And sometimes all or part of a page may be missing from our copy of the book. Or the paper may be so discolored from age that it is difficult to read. We apologize and gratefully acknowledge Google's assistance.

After we re-typeset and design a book, the page numbers change so the old index and table of contents no longer work. Therefore, we often remove them; otherwise, please ignore them.

We carefully proof read any book that will sell enough copies to pay the proof reader; unfortunately, most don't. So instead we try to let customers download a free copy of the original typo-free book. Simply enter the barcode number from the back cover of the paperback in the Free Book form at www.RareBooksClub.com. You may also qualify for a free trial membership in our book club to download up to four books for free. Simply enter the barcode number from the back cover onto the membership form on our home page. The book club entitles you to select from more than a million books at no additional charge. Simply enter the title or subject onto the search form to find the books.

If you have any questions, could you please be so kind as to consult our Frequently Asked Questions page at www.RareBooksClub.com/faqs.cfm? You are also welcome to contact us there.

General Books LLC™, Memphis, USA, 2012.

❦ ❦ ❦ ❦ ❦ ❦ ❦ ❦

HARVARD COLLEGE LIBRARY
FROM
r THE BEQUEST OF
EVERT JANSEN WENDELL
lata

———

M. St. Heran De Montmerin (Governor of Auvergne)

Count De Lanoys (a Huguenot Gentleman at Clermont).

Gaspar De Lomagne (Seigneur de Terignac, attached to the service of the Queen of Navarre).

Henri De Courtines (Son of Count de Courtines).

The Abbe Raimond.

Maitre Laroche (of the Faculty of Poitiers).

Morsau (Secretary to the Governor of Auvergne).

Judges.

Karl Fritz (1st Emissary).

Second Emissary.

Jean Baptiste (1st Gaoler, Palais de Justice, Poitiers).

Andre (2nd Gaoler).

Francois (Servant to Gaspar Lomagne).

Messenger.

Catholics, Huguenot, Servant, etc.

Countess De Lanoys.

Marie De Lanoys (her Daughter).

Marguerite (her Niece).

Gabrielle (Marguerite's Maid).

THE HUGUENOT ACT I.

SCENE I.

Gaspak's Library.

Francois, *his servant, arranging the Table.*

Enter Gabrielle. *Gab.* Ah, Francois! We've heard of your return from Paris, and I am come to know if it be really so. 'Twas thought that you were gone for a year at least, but a month has scarcely passed, and you are here again. *Fran.* Yes, mademoiselle. You see it is impossible to stay away from such attractions as we have here *(patting her on the shoulder).* *Gab.* None of your nonsense, if you please. You had much to do with it, I daresay; but tell me *truly,* what brings you back so soon... tress will be inquisitive when I assure her that you are returned. *Fran.* Truly, then, I do not know; but this I can tell you, very soon after our arrival in Paris a deep gloom came over my master, he suddenly became pensive, neglected his ordinary habits, and ordered me to prepare for our return; and here we are. *Gab.* Poor young man! I daresay something very dreadful has happened to him, for Monsieur the Cure says he is a heretic; and you know what *heretics* are. *Fran.* Why...no...I can't say that I do exactly. *Gab.* Neither do I; but I am sure they must be something very dreadful, for nobody does seem to know just what they are; but when they are caught they are burnt. so they must be *very* bad. *Fran.* For my part, I think they are just as good as we are; only, as you say, they are heretics. But did I tell you, Mademoiselle Gabrielle, I fancy we are leaving again directly? Wait a moment, for I may not see you again before we go. *Exit. Gab.* What! going again! I declare these incessant *goings* are most vexatious. What chance has a poor girl like me of securing a husband, when the man she has set her heart upon is so constantly going going. *(Reenter* Francois.) I am thinking, Francois, how pleasing it must be to run about, as you do, and meet so many damsels *(playing with her fingers and looking at him askance).* I wish mademoiselle would go to Paris, that I might see a little more of the world. *Fran.* And do you desire to see more lads than you have here to flirt with? *Gab.* Well, 'tis very nice, you know, to be made much of. *Fran.* Oh, yes...yes...very *nice...I* find it so when I'm away. *Gab.* But are you sure you're never duped? *Fran.* And if I am...'tis *very* nice, you know, to be made much of, even if it be but for a time. *Gab.* Yes, I find it so when I am told that I'm angelic...and then, you know, 'tis said so seriously, that even if it be a cheat, it pleases for the moment. *Fran. (aside).* The coquette! but I'll be even

with her. *(To Gabrielle.)* Yes...yes *(rubbing his chin)*, for my part, I don't believe in artifice when I see tears accompanying vows of truth...and constancy...and love. *Gab.* Crocodiles, they say, shed tears; and *they* live by *cheating* and *kidnapping.* For my part I'd shed tears for no man. *Fran.* You're quite sure of that? *Gab.* Yes...very sure;...but was it for all this that you asked me to wait for you? *Fran.* N...o...oh, dear no!...You see from some few-words that have fallen from monsieur, I think it very likely we may be away from Clermont...perhaps for a long time...very long...perhaps for ever *(with assumed melancholy)*, and I wanted to say good-bye before parting. *Gab.* It's very thoughtful of you! But I'm scarcely worth the trouble...if my mind is bent on flirting, as you say. *Fran.* Oh, but that was said in jest; and now that we are going, I should like to part as friends—dear friends. You have no idea, Mademoiselle Gabrielle, how charming it is, when one is away, to think of friends at home; and to look up at the moou and stars, and to think that the dearest of them may be looking at them too Then on a
Sunday to go to holy *muss...(taking her hand).* Do you know, I sometimes go because I think you may be going too *(putting his other arm round her waist)*; and then I wonder if you think of me in your prayers, as I often think of you *(Gabrielle crying, and Frangois with his handkerchief wipes away her tears)*? But you are shedding tears, Gabrielle. *Gab.* Oh! oh, no...no...they're not tears. *Fran.* But they are very like tears. *Gab.* *(sobbing)*. It's very hard...and very... very unfair...that you men cau make us shed tears. *Fran.* But if they are a proof of truth and feeling...and...love. *Gab.* I'm sure they are not; for...I...d...o...n. ..'tlove you. *Fran. (kissing her hand).* Don't you, indeed, Gabrielle?
Gab. (still sobbing). No...n...no...no.
Fran. (kissing her cheek). Do you hate me, Gabrielle?
Gab. Yes...s...no...no...no.
Fran. Come, then! one favour more *(kissing her again),* and one that I shall often sigh for...when, looking at the moon and stars, I think of you, dear

Gabrielle, and fancy you may be looking at them too, and sighing like myself *(again kissing her).* *Gab.* For shame! Here comes monsieur *(enter* Gaspar). Good day, monsieur *(courtseying).* *Gasp.* Good day, Gabrielle. Does the Count de Lanoys know that I am again in Clermont? *(During this speech Frangois retires to back of the stage).* *Gab.* I am sent to know if it be really so, monsieur *(courtseying).* *Gasp.* I know that your mistress places her full trust in you *(Gabrielle courtesies)*...Return, and say that I will wait upon her within the next two hours *(giving her a piece of money, and patting her under the chin).* *Gab.* Yes, monsieur. *(Aside.)* I am sure he's no heretic, or if he were I only wish just such another were as fond of me as I am certain he is of Mademoiselle Marguerite. *Exit. Gasp.* Francois *(Frangois approaches),* I have business-which demands my presence in the town; but I must leave again as soon as possible. Let all things be ready, and be prepared yourself; and Francois...I desire'that my arrangements may not be spoken of to anyone. *Fran.* Monsieur's orders shall be obeyed. *Exit. Gasp. (seating himself at the table):*
So, then! The specious treaty, ratified
But two years back, was, indeed, too seemly
To lull suspicion! A gen'ral amnesty,
And free exercise of our religion;
A restoration, too, of property
Confiscated; and four fair towns of France
As hostages, indubious of good faith.
The terms were excellent! So good, in fact,
That they *must* be a snare. Distrust proceeds
From superfluity of kindness;
And we, just now, are so caressed at Court
That I, for one, have taken leave of it.
Enter Count De Lanoys *announced by* Franqois. *Count.* How now, my good friend Gaspar? Your return I've heard of, and I come now to express My wonder that you should be here again So soon. *Gasp.* I am very glad to see you, Count,
But do you really wonder?

Count. Faith, I do;
For Paris now appears to be the heart
Of gaiety. And, since the peace concluded
    At St. Germains, France seems to breathe again.
Gasp. 'Tis just that peace, dear Count, which breeds In those who deeper than the surface look. distrust *Count.* But surely there can be no perfidy
Now that an amnesty has been proclaim'd!
Security, it seems, is doubly sure;
Since envoys have been sent to punish all
Excesses practised upon Huguenots.
Gasp. Listen, dear Count. The tortuous policy
Of Catherine, conjoin'd with that of Rome,
(Each rule being back'd by Philip, King of Spain)
To stamp out the reform'd religion,
Is bearing, even now, its deadly fruit.
The Papal Bull, granting to Charles the power
To alienate the Church's property
To the tune of one hundred thousand crowns,
For prosecuting an unholy war
Against the *heretics,* and utterly
Destroying them, is still in force. At Trent,
In Council 'twas declar'd that faith need not
Be kept with heretics; and, later still,
The doctrine has been taught that massacre
Is just—ay, more,—is useful to salvation.
These pious ordinances have made their mark
Upon the public mind, and taint it still.
The wily Philip's heart is in the plot;
But *his* zeal is curb'd by *temporal* suasion;
The ills of a protracted war forecasting,
He thinks the time may come when France, infirm
By civil feud, and drain'd of her best blood,
May fall an easy prey to his ambition.
At home we've cowardice and perfidy
Reigning supreme; and with them their weapons.

The poison'd chalice, and th' assassin's knife.

Count. If all you say be true, how comes it then
That our most Christian King is now in league
With Louis of Nassau to aid the Prince
Of Orange? And that his sister Margaret,
The Princess of Valois, has been betrothed
To Henry of Navarre? And why, just now,
Are Huguenots the favourites at Court?

Gasp. Tut... tut... dear Count; these are the very By which our godly and *most Christian King* snares Seeks to encompass our destruction. An intercepted letter from the Pope Points to some vile and treacherous scheme, to lure Together all the Huguenots of note In and about the purlieus of the Court. Which being accomplished—well...we know 'tis true, That thick grass is much easier mown than thin. But let us make truce to these forebodings. How fares the Countess? *Count.* Well. *Gasp.* And Marguerite? *Count.* Well too...but somewhat discomposed, I fear By Henri de Courtines, by reason of Some sentiment her father once express'd, At least, so it is said, before he died, (Death's onslaught oft incites foreshadowings) And Courtine's faith, you know, is also hers. *Gasp.* And she? *Count.* Abhors him as a crafty knave,
Yet rather than resentment to provoke
By reason of our being Huguenots—
Gives an unwilling ear, but bars all hope.

Gasp. Go you homeward?
Count. Yes. *Gasp.* Then will I with you For I've already made my coming known.

SCENE II.

A ROOM IN COUNT DE LANOYS' CHATEAU.

A Bouquet of Flowers on the Table. Gaspar *leading in* Marguerite. *Marg,* But when my Cousin Joshua urged your stay, And promised such preferment as it seems His rank and influence might have rendered sure,
Held you his honesty in doubt? *(loth sit down by table.) Gasp.* E'en so.

An upright man may Joshua Barbier be,
But he's a convert; and religious zeal
Most fiercely burns in each new convert's heart.
Well know I the allurements of a Court,
Its fair professions, and its honied words,—
(The serpent's winding 'neath a beauteous flower)
But, Marguerite *(rising),* I've a craving here,
"Which distance sharpens, and which teaches me
That what I thought might be a passing dream,—
A mere caprice,—is pure idolatry.

Marg. What mean you, Gaspar?

Gasp. (taking one of the flowers). Do flowers feel
Their loss when sever'd from the parent stem
That gave them birth, and nourish'd them?

Marg. They must;
Else wherefore droop they, parted from that stem?
And why revive they when they're tended to?
Lifting their leaflets to the cheerful sun,
And from its beams a life restored display?

Gasp. Such flower art thou to me, dear Marguerite!
I saw you drooping when your mother died,
And tears, like dew-drops, starting from your eyes,
Gave beauty to your downcast, opening bloom.
We were *both* children then, and oft did we
Together nestle in our childish play:
Then, as your bosom heaved, I sometimes thought
'Twas in response to mine; for a bright smile
Would—like a sunbeam—rouse your flagging mien,
And kindle up new life. That phantasy
I have indulged, until it has become
An inspiration—a prophetic dream
Foreshadowing two lives.

Marg. It's scarcely fair
To use a stratagem in such a case!

Hearts are not subjects for Diplomacy
To traffic with, although it is just now
The fashion so to make them.

Gasp. Pardon, dear,
The rooted usage of my avocation,
Heaven knows! I would not gain an inch of ground
By tortuous course. Yet you will not ask me
A word that I have uttered to retract?

Marg. I own that when I think upon our games
In former times,—as oft I do,—they seem
Like shadows cast before a blissful life.

Gasp. And dare I hope they may be so?

Marg. Caspar,
I'll throw aside all maiden reticence,
And own to you that every word you've breathed
Seems but the echo of an inward voice
Which bids me vow / *love you* with a faith
Trustful as that with which the sailor clings
To his frail bark when angry waves grow high
And threaten him; yet knows he that he's safe.

Gasp. What music do I hear? or do I dream? *Marg.* I'm told, you know, that 'twas my father's Express'd before he died—that I should wed hope—— The son of Count de Courtines, who, of late With importunity has urged his suit; (More to my aunt, however, than to me) But,—from his kinship with the Count de Retz, A favourite at Court—my guardians here Being Huguenots—— I have restrain'd my tongue From any word that could resentment stir; But, oh! the joy to expatiate on my love Is more than I have power to express. Am I too bold, dear Gaspar? If so it be, I will be charier of my tenderness. Or if my speech o'erstep a maiden's rule, I will retract my words;—but that I may Repeat, and still repeat, them o'er again. *Gasp.* Heaven bless thee, dearest! The temptation's For I should never tire of hearing them; great, But I will curb the fancy, since it needs A recantation of your precious vow; And I have much upon my mind to say. You ask'd me whether I thought Barbier true, And I replied by saying he's a *convert*. Restraint on liberty of conscience Is the main dogma he has preached of late, And it is one that with his early training Is at strange variance. Yet he points to me

As a fit envoy to the Hollander! The mission I'd accept,—but it demands

loo long a stay in Paris;—which just now

Is perilous and bodes no good.

Marg. You speak

Mysteriously; yet have I sometimes thought, From many late events, that much which you Have hinted at may be too true; but these Are things on which I dare not question you.

Gasp. Nay, ask me, dearest, what you will; for not

Without cause have I ask'd myself; and I

Have answers by the score which prove my charge.

Our foe shrinks not from crime and perfidy In every act and deed with Huguenots. The use of cunning poisons reigns supreme; Inquisitors have craftily devised A fiendish judgment seat—a court of blood— Wherein e'en virtues have been made false pleas For deeds of guilt; and Heaven's fair name invoked, To vindicate the acts.

Marg. My daily converse

With my guardians here has made me ponder Much on many of these things; but I have Hoped that they were of the past, and changed For deeds attesting confidence and trust.

Gasp. Would that it were so! But e'en now I'm With business at Rochelle, which may avert charged A cruel blow that's aimed at Huguenots. My charge, mind you, befits a patriot's aim,

And I must leave thee for a time—meanwhile—

I *could not* quit this spot without the delve Into your very soul, which I have made, To seek an interchange of vows—before

We part. Say! you will not deem it selfish?

Marg. Think you 'tis selfish of the youth who goes Where duty calls him forth,—to plight his *word,* His *honour,* and his *love,* to her whom he May never meet again? But is it true That we must really part?

Gasp. I fear it is;

But for a time—a little time I trust.

Enter Gabrielle. *Gab.* Monsieur de Montmerin is in the salon, where the countess begs the favour of mademoiselle's presence. *Marg.* I come, Gabrielle. *Exit* Gab. You go at once you say r

Gaspar *bows assent.*

I shall hear of you? *from you? must* you go?

Gasp. Be very sure thou wilt be well inform'd Of each and every move that I may make; Perchance th' adoption of some other name Prudence may call for whilst I am away; But of all this anon. Bless thee, dearest; And may Heaven's blessing go along with mine! Once more, farewell, and henceforth when I crave A moment's bliss, my thoughts will turn to thee As truly as the needle to the pole; Good bye, sweet heart.

Marg. A thousand times good bye.

SCENE III. SALON IN THE SAME CHATEAU.

Count *and* Countess De Lanoys, M. De Montmerin *and*

Marie. *Mont.* It is a privilege of office such As that I hold, to mitigate the blow Which must be felt by thousands, in a case Like this; and so far as condolence goes,

And fellow feeling can a wound assuage, His Majesty the King commands me give Th' assurance of his royal sympathy.

Countess. It is very sudden! scarce two short weeks In Paris; and in full health!—as 'twas thought— Was her son with her?

Mont. I know not, but 'tis said An overtaxed brain has been the cause.

Enter Marguerite.

Ah, mademoiselle! Lovely as ever! And as gracious! How charming would it be If every face we meet—in this low world— Were fashioned like to yours!

Marg. You flatter, sir; And what a world 'twould be if every tongue Were given—as yours is now—to flattery!

Countess. His Excellency, Marguerite, has come To announce the death of Her Majesty The Queen of Navarre.

Marg. (aghast). Of whom?

Countess. Of the Queen Of Navarre.

Marg. Impossible! four or five Days since she was alive—and well in health— I know she was—But...oh... What do I say? I must have dreamt as much...and yet...I feel It's all...as-..if... (stagers *and Jails fainting in a chair. Marie rushes up to her, whilst the Count exclaims) Count.* Who's there? *Marie.* Marguerite speak! I pray you speak!—she is not given to faint,—

Enter Servant.

Count. Some water—quick.

Exit Servant, *and re-enters with water, which the* Count *sprinkles on* Marguerite's *face, who gradually revives, looks about her, and fixes her eyes on* Mont. *Marie.* See! she revives—oh, speak! *Marg.* Pardon me, my friends... I have been lately Indisposed...Who did you say was dead? *Count. (aside).* The darling child! *Mont. aside).* She cannot doubt the Of our dispatches!—But why this flutter? truth *Countess.* His Excellency,

child, has kindly come
To give us tidings of the sudden death
Of one who was Queen of Navarre.
Marg.

    The Queen

      Of Navarre! O my head!—The sudden death...

When did she die? How very strange that I

Should feel so ill! But it is passing now!
(To Mont.) I know you will excuse me—will you not?

Pray let me to my chamber go, dear aunt.
Marie. I'll take you, cousin. But, oh! how you have Frightened me!
Mont.. Stir not, mademoiselle;

For I will leave you with your friends. Later

In the day I will inquire concerning you—

To the pleasure of our next meeting.
Count. (conducting him to the door).
I thank your Excellency...au revoir. *Exit*
Mont.
Marie. Oh, dear! oh, dear! How glad I am he's gone?

And yet 'twas gracious that he first did come

To us! How goes it now, dear Marguerite?
Marg. Thanks Marie...better...yet I greatly fear

That I have play'd the fool...But why disguise?

Dearest aunt—I pray you write directly
To Gaspar, and inform him of the news.
Pray let Gabrielle be the bearer of it.
The intelligence—if he knows it not
Already—his arrangements may alter;
Of which, when you have done, I will apprize you.
Marie. What cunning spell has worked this change, *Marg. (inquiringly).* I am not changed...am I?
Marie. But yesterday I could have sworn that you

Were proof 'gainst any such surprise as that

Which now disturbs you...Has Gaspar whispered

In your ear, as men do into horses,
When they would subdue them?
Marg. 'Tis true. I am

    Confused with thoughts which my

untutor'd mind
'Till now has laughed at. Now they perplex me.

Yet are they very joyous? But you love
Gaspar...Marie...do you not?
Marg. No...no...say not with all your soul! Leave such A measure of devotion to me, dear;

    With all my soul.

    To whom, in truth, he has revealed his love,

As I have mine to him.
Marie. I guess'd as much.

    And *must* you come to me at last to be Admonished on such nonsense?
(leading Marg. out with her arm round her waist, and aside) ...'tis very nice though!

SCENE IV. IN THE SUBURB OF CLERMONT.

M. De Montmerin *meeting* M. Henri De Courtines. *Mont.* Well met, Courtines. How goes it? and what *Court.* Eain would I ask your excellency that. news?
Mont. Well, I've just left a scene concerning which You may, perhaps, enlighten me somewhat. *Court.* Is't so, indeed? And what may be the gist? *Mont.* Within these two hours missives have arrived

Bearing from Paris the announcement of

The sudden death of Jeanne, Queen of Navarre.
Court. (with affected surprise).
Heaven save the mark! But how say they she died?
Mont. (affecting not to regard the question).
Presuming that th' event might interest
The Count and Countess de Lanoys, at once

I hastened to them to impart the news.
Their charming niece, on hearing of th' event

With much emotion sank into a swoon.
Her sense returning, forth she stammered words,

Uttered at random, yet which made it clear

That, *to her,* much import had the tidings.
Court. Excess of feeling, doubtless, was the cause. *Mont.* Granted. But in this case may it not be

That such excess of feeling has its source

In some soul-stirring recess of the heart
Wherein a potent monarch rules supreme?
Court. What other monarch than her woman's soul? *Mont.* Well...this youthful Seigneur de Terignac,

Gaspar Lomagne, has been an attache,
A favourite, too, 'tis said, of the late queen.
Court. And what do you infer from that? *Mont.* But this,

May there not be some blandishment... ay, more...

Some tender sympathetic chord, between

This Gaspar Lomagne and fair Marguerite?
Court. No...no...her destiny is link'd with mine.
Mont. Ay? But are you her accepted suitor? *Court.* If I am not, still there remains the fact That on his death-bed 'twas her father's wish That we should be united. *Mont.* Be not so sure, then.

The wish, you say, her father once express'd

Was coined, perchance, within the haze of death,

When you were both in leading strings. But now

She has the mind to cater for herself.
The seigneur is grown a noble fellow,
A Huguenot, 'tis true, but all men have
Their failings; and his sit so well on him,

That I like him all the better for them;
And so does someone else, or I misjudge.

Nor should I be surprised to hear that he
Has the adhesion of the family council
To second him.
Court. A very noble fellow!

    But with unbounded impudence, it seems,

To come between the girl and me; besides,

He is, as you observe, a Huguenot
And she a Catholic.
Mont. Pin not your faith

    On such an obstacle; for, after all,
The difference may not be so very great
As many of us think, when love steps in
To bridge it over.

Court. I'll fight the fellow.

Mont. But, as a swordsman, are you quite his match? Think well of that. He's skilful in most things. *Court.* That question, certainly, deserves due thought; Yet may I trap him. For I have letters

From the Count de Retz, setting forth that he

Prom Paris has, j ust now, escaped by stealth,

Without the license of His Majesty;

For as an envoy to the Netherlands

He was approved. For this apostacy

It is deemed expedient his proceedings

Should be duly watched and reported on.

Mont. Surely you would not play the spy, would you?

Court. Oh, no! Certainly not...but...

Mont. But what? Say— *Court.* "Well, then...you think he has supplanted me?

Mont. And if he has, will you retaliate With base infamy? Swallow your grievance, If it should be one; but at the sword's point Seek not your remedy... I distrust you. *Court.* But how am I to act? *Mont.* Act like a man;

Divert your thoughts; that's not a hard thing now.

These are strange times; and be assured that what

You've thought a link has never had a place,

At least, within her breast.

Court. 'Tis galling though

   To be defeated by a heretic.

And on a point involving self-esteem!

You would not have me grieve if, by some chance,

He were attainted for his stealthy flight.

And so an end to his philandering made.

Mont. Perhaps; but if you have regard for her,

That which you would should be no act of yours,

Neither should you therewith connected be.

'Tis clear that you a shadow have pursued,

And shadowlike it has escaped you.

But let us change our talk. Who have we here?

Taking the arm of Courtines, *and observing* Gaspar

and FRANgois *entering towards them, disguised*

as magicians, each carrying a divining rod,

Gaspar *applying his to the ground, it stands erect.*

   What do you here with your divining rod?

For such I deem it is as you now use it.

Gaspar. Tush...tush.. see you not sympathetic force As now my magic wand turns here and there. Such subtle matter lies commixed therein That in the hands of an adept 'twill turn On all things which evoke man's weal or wee. O'er mines and water it will stand erect; Prom thieves and miscreants 'twill averted turn; On landmarks mov'd by stealth, it will incline Towards the right and ever shuns the wrong.

Court. (looking suspiciously at Gaspar). How stands it, sir, affected when 'tis brought Into close contact with a Huguenot?

Codnt De Lanoys entering. Count. That question may at once be solved by me: For I'm a subject...as you know...to test it. niece?

Mont. Ah, Count! how fares it now with your fair *Count.* I thank you...well...but how about the rod? *Mont.* Our friend here has a hazel of great power;

But questions such as that of man's belief

Our conscience answers better than a rod.

Exeunt Montmerin, De Courtines, *and the* Count

following them/ but Gaspar *pulls him by his*

dress and signals him to remain—the Count *astonished.*

Count. What would you with me, sir? I know you not. *Gaspar. (looking anxiously that no one overhears).* My garb is perfect then as a disguise. *(Disclosing himself.) Count.* Gaspar! Is't you? What means this mas querade? *Gaspar.* I've heard, dear Count, of all that has transAnd I must hence to La Rochelle. Therefrom pired, I may induce Coligny and the king To place themselves in safety. The late queen, Whose death we

mourn, was feared by Catherine, And so is now Coligny, on whose life Murd'rous attempts have more than once been made. In 1566 the Prince de la Roche informed Coligny that at a secret Council it had been resolved to arrest the Prince de Conde and himself (Coligny); to imprison the prince for life, and to bring Coligny to the

The time and circumstances are mature

To gain for France his best and dearest hopes

To cast aside th' oppressive yoke of Spain.

And from the crafty Philip take the sting,

By an alliance 'with the English Court;

These things may best be done at La Rochelle.

My steps are being dogged, and therefore 'tis

I need disguise to penetrate the ranks

Of Anjou's army, which lies on my road.

I'm told my flight from Paris is unwise,

But I would rather save my life with fools

Than forfeit it with those who are o'erwise.

Count. Your project, as I understand it, is

So to avert all scrutiny from yourself

To that for treasures lying underground

Whilst you your course unheeded may pursue.

Gaspar. So tend both my disguise and stratagem

For each inspires men with the greed of gain,

And to all other senses blinds their eyes;

So now adieu! As a disciple, I

Of Cochlinius the famed necromancer;

And Francois, my serving man in magic,

Our fortunes cast on these poor hazel twigs.

scaffold. Subsequently an attempt was made to poison Coligny, and the criminal was bis own valet, who confessed the crime before he was hanged.

ACT II.

SCENE I.

A ROOM IN MONSIEUR DE Montmerin's HOTEL.

   Montmerin *with his Secretary* Morsau. *Mont.* These nuptials 'twixt young Henri de Beam And Marguerite de Valois appear, forsooth, To have been celebrated with the pomp And circumstance of a royal marriage. Pope Gregory has been, as it appears, Less obdurate than his predecessor, In granting the dispensation: although 'Tis said the queen has cut the Gordian knot, By fabricating what the Pope refused. A clever woman, that! Subtle, perhaps, History will judge her. That is to say, She well knows how occasions to improve. This marriage, if it serve no other end, Is the best answer to the lawless power Which, with high hand, the house of Guise usurps. And should restore tranquillity to France And cause less need of Spain.

Mor. The service here
Should be less onerous. Heaven knows! we need
A truce to the conflicting doubts and fears
Which keep all minds, at present, on the stretch.—
For nights past I have had such stirring dreams,
That they have raised in me a strange desire
To join the students in the Pre-aux-Clercs,
As was my wont when I was one of them.

Mont. Go...by all means go...The time is fitting:
For you will have the opportunity
Of joining in the revels of the Court.

Enter Servant. *Sent.* A messenger bearing dispatches from Paris would see your Excellency. *Mont.* Bid him enter.

Exit Servant, *who returns with* Messenger. *Messr.* I am commanded, sir,
By the Count de Retz, to place this letter In your Excellency's hands.

Mont. Good... good...
You may retire, and order such repast As, doubtless, you must need. *Exit* Messenger.
What have we here?
A Royal dispatch it seems; at least it bears
The Royal Seal. *(Opens and reads.)*
To his Excellency Monsieur St. Heran De Montmerin.

Sir,—I am commanded by His very High and Powerful Majesty to inform you of a conspiracy, which appears to have originated and to have been organised by His Majesty's subjects of the Reformed Religion against His Royal Person; and I am furthermore charged to inform you of the retaliatory measures which it has been deemed advisable to adopt, by His Majesty in Council, for the better security of the Royal Family and of the country in general. The plot seems to have such extended ramifications that nothing short of an absolute extermination of the Huguenots appears likely to accomplish the end. Grievous as it is to our Sovereign Master to enjoin such massacre, it is His Majesty's Royal will that no mercy be shown to those of His Majesty's subjects who profess the Religion of the Huguenots. Wherefore you are charged by His Majesty to assist by the aid of Emissaries, who will be directed to act under you, in such work of destruction in the Province of Auvergne, to which you are accredited; and as a warranty, in vindication of any and every such act, His Majesty has attached his Royal Seal hereunto.

I have the honour to be. Monsieur, your obedient servant, De Retz. *Morsau.* Horrible!

Monl. It must be a fabrication!
So adverse is it to my charge of peace *(considers)*
I will renounce the missive. You, my friend,
Shall be the bearer of my answer. Write—
(morsau *writes as* Montmerin *dictates.*)

Sire,—I have received a message under your Majesty's Hand and Seal to put to death all Huguenots within this Province. I respect your Majesty too much to suppose the letter to be other than a forgery; but if (which God forbid) such commands have emanated from your Majesty, I have still too much esteem for you to obey it. With profound respect, I have the honour to be, Sire, your Majesty's most humble and devoted servant and subject,

St. Heran De Montmerin. *(Aside)* I would not that my faith and loyalty Were shaken by vain doubts; and yet this charge
Cannot be unprompted; *(to* Morsau) Morsau, tell me,
How quickly will you be prepared to leave?

Morsau. This very hour, if it so please you, sir.

Mont. Be it so, and the messenger shall be
Your escort. From this letter I suppose It may not be quite safe to go alone.
(Rings bell. Servant *enters.)*
Pray bring the Messenger again to us.
Exit Servant. *Morsau.* I have no fear.
Re-enter Messenger. *Mont.* I shall again require
Your services a few hours hence, to act
As an escort to this gentleman, straight To Paris.

Messr. I will be prepared forthwith;
But 'twill be well, before we start, that he
Should be provided with a scarf, like this.
(Taking a white scarf from his pocket.)
Mont. To what intent?
Messr. I'm told it is a charm.
When tied around the sleeve it has the power
To turn aside the bullets and the blades "Which have of late in Paris havoc made.
At all events, 'twill do no harm. It may Save us much trouble, and protect us, too,
From danger.

Mont. 'Tis well. As you have used it, The like precaution shall be now observed.

Messr. Would your Excellency see two persons, Who have accompanied me from Paris?

Mont. Who are they? *Messr.* They are instructed—say they—
To impart to you alone their errand. the suspicions *Mont.* Let them come. *Exit* Messenger. Morsau, if Which have of late obtain'd expression here, Touching the motives that do sway the King, To lure the Huguenots about the Court, Be, by the current of events, con fumed, I shall be after you right soon, in Paris.
Enter Karl Fritz *and* 2nd Emissary—*introduced by* Servant, *who retires. Karl.*

Your servant, sir. May our interview
with Your Excellency be strictly pri-
vate? *(looking at* Morsatj*)*. *Mont.* Cer-
tainly. Morsau, my good friend, will jou
Leave us for a time? *Exit Morsau. Karl.*
I am commanded
To wait the pleasure of your Excellency
For such instructions, as in obedience
To a letter just now delivered to you,
By my friend, the Messenger, from
Paris,
You may impart. Selection has been
made
Of agents to the Governor of Auvergne,
By reason of the knowledge we possess
Of the chief Huguenots in the purlieus
here—
And in the Province.
Mont. May I ask from whom
   You have your orders?
Karl. The letter, I was told,
Would fully solve all that; and so place
us
   At once in union with your Excellen-
cy.
Mont. And am I then to understand that
you,
Of your free will, accept so vile a rdle;
By words too horrible to be expressed?
Karl. Well it is not just the occupation
That one would fix upon for its repute;
But crops some weeding need, from
time to time;
And, I suppose, that human nature
grows
The better, also, from such timely tend-
ing.
Such is the light in which we have been
taught
To look upon our present business.
Mont. Have you, then, practised it al-
ready?
Karl. Why...yes...We came but now in
contact with The Admiral Coligny...The
Duke de Guise Gave him his *coup de
grace.*—So you perceive We do our
work in famous company. *Mont.* What!
The Admiral Coligny killed? *Karl.* E'en
so.
Two days before, a bungler shot at him,
And on the morrow—greeted by the
King—
So great his pain, that 'twas perhaps
thought good,
And kindly, too, to free him from it all.

Mont. Good God! and is it come to this?
Look you,
Return to those who have employed
you,
And let them know that there are other
means,
If not less vile—more manly in their
show—
Than delegating into murd'rous hands
The worst of crimes. Of what Province
are you?
Karl. From Lorraine.
Mont. A fitting place! and as such
You may perhaps feel bound to serve
the House
Of Guise. Go to them and give my mes-
sage
As I have given it you. Naught will I
have
To do with paid assassins....There's the
door—
And the sooner you're away from Cler-
mont
The better will it be for you.
Exeunt Emissaries *with assumed indig-
nation.* SCENE II.

   A WOODED WALK NEAR CLERMONT.
   Marguerite *and* Marie *seated under
a tree. Marie.* Do you know—dear
Cousin—I find your friend, The Abbe
Raimond, most agreeable.
Marg. So good, too—is he not? A bish-
opric,
I have heard, has been accorded to him,
And—for conscience sake—he has re-
fused it.
Marie. No!—fancy our familiar gossip-
ing!
With a potential bishop, too. And what
A white aristocratic hand he has!
The pastoral ring will well become it.
Marg. Ere he came here, 'tis said, soci-
ety
Was dull and stupid; but 'tis not so now,
For ladies flock to his confessional,
And he makes *men* to love religion.
Marie. I admire him much; albeit won-
der how
Ladies can ever take up with a priest.
I like the Abbe very much but yet—
   Somehow—I can't imagine what it is
   Now, I know you're going to laugh at
me *Marg.* Why should I? I admire him,
too...and yet... I do not—as you say—
take up with him.

Marie. Well, priests don't seem to be
exactly like
To other men...They have no beard, you
know.
Marg. As for that, some other men are
beardless;
And you'll *admit* that Madame Valerie
Has a prodigious beard; a moustache,
too.
Marie. Her chin is very fertile. Still it's
not
A *manly beard.* It seems to come and
go.
It gives you not the sentiment of
strength,
And *manly daring.. .*such as soldiers
have.
In fact, I think of it as nothing.
A priest might have just such another
beard
And yet be no less priestly in his looks.
Marg. You'll confess, it is an ugly noth-
ing!
She dresses well, however, and e'en
that's
A virtue when it fails to be an instinct.
But behold!...Who have we here ap-
proaching?
Let us withdraw...I know them not..-do
you?
*The Ladies retire to a covert path be-
hind brushwood. Enter* Karl Fritz *and*
2nd Emissary. *2nd Emis.* Our business
here has chafed the Governor. Albeit
the source from which our orders come.
Karl. It cannot be denied that we are
knaves,
But circumstances in this wicked world
Reconcile better men to evil ways;
And our's are not the cleanest.—But
this is
Neither the time nor place to scrutinize
Our motives: therefore let us to our
work.
Now there's one Gaspar de Lomagne,
whose hash
I'd gladly settle for him; for it seems
(marguerite *appears listening)*
That he and Lignerolles knew of the
plot
   Contemplated; and from the very lips
   Of Anjou's Duke. Lignerolles has
disappeared.
(Making signs to the earth.) To send
Lomagne to keep him company. Would

be a master-stroke of policy, Likely to
be appreciated too;

And our affairs here greatly simplified.
of him *2nd Emis.* Lomagne...Lomagne.
..sure that's the name *(Pulling out a
note-book and conning it).*

Whose whereabouts we were to ascertain;

And from the very man with whom
we have

A rendezvous here...Ay, it is even so.
(Reading " Mons. de Courtines will instruct you how

To approach one Sieur Lomagne, at
Clermont."

Here comes our friend I trow. Now
for the sign.
*(Both putting a white handkerchief
round their arms).*

I hope he'll prove more docile than
the governor.
(Enter De Courtines *cautiously). Court.*
From Paris I presume...May I inquire
Your business here, and by whom you
are sent? *Karl.* This letter will explain
our business; and *(Giving a letter to*
Courtines)
As you may see...'tis from the Count de
Hetz.
Court. (opening the letter and reading.)
Yes...yes...I see it is the counterpart
Of one I've lately had...The messenger,——
By your presence here,—has done my
bidding.
What kind of help do you require from
me?
Karl. But little...very little...for we have
A list of those to whom our *attention*
Should be chiefly given. Yet are there
some
Whose liberation from all worldly cares
Might gratify the Court. One above
all,——
The Sieur Lomagne...Gaspar...Lomagne...whose past
In the House of Navarre, gives him importance
At La Rochelle, where danger is most
feared.
Court. And what would you from me
concerning him? *Karl.* Only instruct us
how we may approach him, And leave
the rest to us. *Court. (after hesitation).*
I'll think of it. But we may be observed;

aud better 'tis We were not seen together. To-morrow, At this hour, and on the
road to Pontgiband, Some half league
hence, I'll meet you. There we may Retire into a mountain glen...fearless Of all
observers. In the mean time I'll Ponder
o'er my kinsman's letter. Go you Your
ways, and I'll go mine...Until to-morrow. *Exeunt Messengers. On going* Karl
*looks for a moment suspiciously behind
the bushwood where the ladies are, but
they are supposed to be wellnigh out
of sight.* (de Courtine *seats himself under the tree, musing).* "The thing you
would should be no act of yours," So
said my friend Montmerin.—Nor would
it If accomplish'd by these men. He further said—"Nor should you be connected with it."—Well! If I describe the
cover of the wolf Surely I'm not connected with the chase
That makes him bite the dust.—Then..."
all's fair,"
'Tis said, "in love and war." And am I
not
Warring with one? And love I not the
girl?
Therefore 'tis doubly fair. And we are
taught,
That " faith with heretics need not be
kept."
Then as a heretic it is...and not
As rival that I will now unearth him.
rising.
No other could it be than this same
man
Whom late I saw disguised in magic
robe.
When *last* seen he was on La
Kochelle road,
From Brioux, so his whereabouts is
sure. *Exit.* (marguerite *advances leading* Marie *by the hand.) Marg.* Marie...
dear Marie...know you the import Of all
that we've been forced to overhear?
Marie. Would, cousin darling! that I did
not know,
Nor do I all; but from those horrid men
This much I gather; that they're on the
track
Of your devoted Gaspar. But wherefore?
Marg. Chiefly, I fear, because of his religion.
And therein you'll have fellow-feeling

with him—
As I have from my very soul. But why
That dastard Courtines should pursue
him so,
Is more than I can comprehend; unless
I am the cause...God in His mercy will
not,
I know, permit such baseness to prevail;
Nor will He fail—in human aid—to turn
Aside their plotting...Marie...let us to
The governor of the province, and lay
Before him all that we have seen and
heard...
I've confidence in his judgment, although
Sometimes he is severe.
Marie. The very thing
To do! For he will best advise us how
To act against these cowardly assassins;
And we shall gain a day on them. Oh,
dear!
Oh, dear! I wish I were a man just now
That I might beard them in their very
dens.
Marg. Perhaps 'tis better as it is; for
woman's
Wit, more than manly strength, doth oft
upset
The foulest machinations. Let's away.
Exeunt.
SCENE III.
(same As 1st Scene or Act 2.)
M. De Montmerin *at a Table Reading.*
Enter Servant *followed by* Marguerite
and Marie. *Servant.* The Demoiselles de
Lanoys, your Excellency.
Exit. Mont. Welcome. But now a dark
and heavy cloud
Hung o'er me, and you come to brighten it—
(Taking both hands of Marguerite.)
Tell me, however—why this pallid
face?
And hands that tremble as do aspen
leaves?
Marg. Pardon, dear sir, this sudden and
abrupt
Intrusion on your privacy. We come
To tell you of foul deeds, which even
now
Are being devised; but, by your aid, we
hope
May be averted. At most an hour ago,
When we were on the road to Pontgiband,

By chance we were constrained to over-
hear
The converse of two men, whose busi-
ness here
Is nothing less than murder.
Mont. I've seen them,
And thought the miscreants safely out
of Clermont.
Marg. looking much astonished).
But what is more Monsieur des
Courtines join'd
Them, and he, as it appears, has tracked
The Sieur Lomagne as far as La
Rochelle,
And there he purposes to send these
men
To entrap and kill him.
Mont. Impossible! *Marie.* Yet said he as
much; and is to meet them On the same
road, some half league from the town.
To-morrow morning. *Mont.* Is it so, in-
deed?
Be sure then I will have a trusty witness
Of their meeting...And, three being in
the plot
'Twill go hard if I know not the very
sum
    And substance of their project. In the
mean time.
My dear young ladies, go you home
forthwith,
Inform your friends of all that has tran-
spired.
Your friendship with the Bishop and the
Abbe
Will guarantee *your* safety. This affair
May here detain me a few hours, after
which
I go to Poitiers, where I have business
Of some import. Dispatch a messenger
With all haste to Rochelle; advise your
friend
There of his jeopardy; urge him at once
To come to me at Poitiers;—there we'll
stay
Together till all danger has blown o'er.
Marg. Thanks—a thousand thanks; we
knew that you Comfort and direct us.
All shall be done would As you advise.
SCENE IV.

A SUBURBAN CABARET.

Men drinking at a table on one side.
Karl *and Marguerite's* Messenger *at a
table on the opposite side by themselves. Messr. (half tipsy to* Karl). It

seems to...m...me...my...my friend...
you're...ve... ve...ry...tipsy... You...you.
.. s...seem to be...here...here...a...and...
th...there...and... e...v...ery...w...where...
I...I...could...under...s...stand... e..very...
thing...you...s... said...but...n... now... I.
.. can't...you...m...must be...v...very...t...
tipsy...and th... that...that is very wrong.
..you know. *Enter* 2nd Emissary. *Karl
(rising and going to meet him).*
Here you are then! It's just as I supposed.
When left you Clermont?
2nd Emiss. Early this morning. *Karl.*
And saw you our friend Courtines ere
you left? *2nd Emiss.* Oh yes. He's bent
on giving all the aid He can in our pur-
suit. *Karl.* But our plans are
Changed; and I will tell you all about
them.
On parting with our pliant friend,
Courtines,
Methought that in the background I per-
ceived
The faintest shadow of a petticoat;
Yet said I naught, for well I knew if we
A listener had, some action would en-
sue;
To thwart the which our scheme re-
quired a change.
I therefore judged that you should meet
Courtines
As was appointed, both at time and
place;
Whilst I—with tidings equal to his
own—
Knew well our game was safe at La
Rochelle.
'Twas needful then—to stop the way of
news
'Twixt him and Clermont. No device
but that
Could so securely bring him in our
clutch.
(The powers above—or those below—
send help
To those who help themselves. Speed
waits on us.)
When two short leagues from Clermont
I'd achieved,
This fellow here o'ertook me on the
road;
And with scant guidance, in his bab-
bling mood,
He told me he was bound for La

Rochelle.
I answer made that I was going there
too,
And on our way I urged him stay to eat,
Which being done, I plied him well with
wine.
He then imparted all I wished to know:
That he the bearer was of a dispatch.
I saw him often fumble at his arm,
And, when he lost all sense, I felt there
too,
And found the letter carefully con-
cealed,
Bound round his arm:—'twas from a la-
dy friend.
I took it to an artful scrivener,
Who, with much skill, a fac-simile
made—
Save that Lomagne is therein urged to
go
To one hotel at Poitiers, where he'll fall
Into the Inquisition's playful hands,
Instead of that where he'd protection
find,
With our indignant friend—the Gover-
nor.
The substituted letter, like the first,
I've bound around the arm of the poor
wretch
Who's still half drunk; but, when him-
self again,
We'll hasten his departure on his er-
rand.
2nd Emiss. Excellent! i' faith, such
management as this Should raise us on
the ladder of promotion.
Karl. Our business now is clearly at
Poitiers,
For there must we a fit reception make
For this well-favoured Seigneur de
Terignac.
The holy Inquisition will—no doubt—
By its own gentle and persuasive acts,
Relieve us of all further thought of him.
'Tis well to have one's dirty work so
done.
Messr. (rising and going up to 2nd
Emissary). Your s...servant, sir. *(To
Karl).* It's time, I think, m...my friend.
..t...that w...we were travelling. *Karl.* I
think so too; but henceforth I must take
Another route, and so must say adieu.
Be very sure you do not drink too much,
But, with befitting speed, your letter
bear,

And show yourself a trusty messenger. *Messenger.* I will...I will...and thank... thank you... for your company so far. ..Good...good day...sir. *Exit, carefully feeling his left arm. Karl.* Good day, my friend, and no more toping, mind, Untjl you reach Rochelle...So, now he's gone. And little, trow I, does the lady dream The pious end to which her missive tends. Come let's away to meet our liege at Poitiers. *2nd Emiss.* Lead on... I'm with you, noble chieftain. SCENE V. DRAWING ROOM IN COUNT DE LANOYS' CHATEAU.

Countess De Lanoys *at a spinning wheel on one side.* Count De Lanoys *seated near her.* Marguerite *and* Marie *arranging flowers at a table on the opposite side.* Marie *with her back to the centre. Window looking out to the Place. Count.* How changed the town within these few days Men look askance at men, with doubtful eyes; past!

And silence reigns, as calm precedes a storm;

And little boots it to our peace of mind That we ourselves are safe. *Countess.* But surely 'tis

A solace to feel one's-self in safety, When angry men pursue a lawless course It is, perhaps, a badge of cowardice; But I confess myself a coward. *Count.* A very charming and a graceful one;

I must admit you look quite beautiful To-day. *Countess (complacently).* And therein, too, I am a I dare not face the ravages of time, coward;

And deem it no great sin to use the arts Which most conceal them. *Marg.* Say, rather, you are

Brave, dear aunt, for, certes, if ravages there are, You do accept them with so good a grace, That—unlike others —you do not disguise Your years, but meet each following one with joy. *Countess.* Alas! alas! it cannot be avoided.

Then why not hide it witli the very hue

(Pointing to herpowdered hair.) Which it inflicts upon us? *Marie (clapping her hands).* Bravo, mamma! That's what 1 call attacking the enemy With his own weapons. *Count.* How about the odds?

Ten to one on the enemy say I. *Marg.* But valour, surely, gains in excellence By the very odds against it pitted. *Marie.* Hurrah then for the weapons! vive la guerre! *Enter* Servant. *Servant.* Monsieur de Courtines. *Count (hesitating).* Give him admission...Some modeLadies, pray. Be composed, dear Marguerite; ration, We have the advantage of knowing him. *Enter* Courtines. *Court.* Ladies, I have the honour to salute you.

Count, how goes it? This popular emeute Troubles you not, I hope..."I/is very sad To see the country turu'd so topsy turvy. *Count.* Still more to feel it breed distrust 'twixt friend And friend. Think you not so? *Court.* Yes, yes. Doubt is Contagious, and the very air seems loaded With it. The Countess, though, is far too good To feel a taint of it. *Countess.* My faith is great,

And, here, we feel it spread, as doubt, you say does. But after all, 'tis hard to counterfeit True friendship; think you not so Monsieur Courtines? *(Looking intently at him.)* *Court.* I doubt not, Countess, that it may be so. *Moving to the Table towards the back* of Marie, *who is unconscious of his approach, and is fitting a coronet of flowers on* Marguerite. *Marie.* How coyly on their drooping stems do these Sweet roses woo thee, dearest Marguerite! *Court.* And well accord too with her beauteous face! (makie *suddenly starts round astonished.) Marg. (addressing herself to* Makie). Would it not fitting be to add thereto A little cypress, or a few immortelles? Do you like immortelles, sir? *To* De Couktines. *Court.*

Why ask you? Emblems of mourning cannot well be *liked,* For as such symbols, do they not give pain? *Marg.* But there's a spell in pain which bids us look Into ourselves, to see how much we've wronged The better portion of our inborn nature. I know a deep-read man whose cunning runes, And magic rites disclose the very soul And tell such tales were better left untold. But *you...*sir...have *no* demon in *your* breast, *No friendly* instinct to let others strike Where you withhold your hand. *Court.* You are severe

In straiuing thus the cynic's view of friendship. But, as it frets not *us,* we need not wince. *(Aside)* Yet will I be revenged, for now I feel How like's the sweet of hate to that of love. *(Enter* Servant *with letter.) Servant.* A courier, sir, brings this letter from Poitiers, from Monsieur the Governor of Auvergne. *Count.* A letter from our good friend Montmerin.

To Countess. *Court. (seeing the agitation of all).* Mesdames and Count I have the honour to wish you a good day. *Exit. The Ladies gather round the* Count, *whilst he opens and reads the letter. Count (reading).* My dear Count,—Our young friend Lomagnes has, by some inconceivable mischance, fallen into the hands of the Inquisition, here at Poitiers. I pray you come with all haste, as his case will be transferred to the secular Court, where your presence may be of service to him. Seeing that it may be necessary for you to stay some time, perhaps you will bring the ladies with you. Depend upon my services for all that I can do. Your devoted, Montmerin. *Marg.* Great God! What do I hear? A prisoner! Under the Inquisition too! What fraud— What diabolic snare has lured him there? And into such a pitfall! *Sits down in despair. Count.* 'Twould

seem, indeed,
That some foul play's at work...
Courtines *must* have
A hand in this! His visit here! His port!
His restless manner...and his sudden flight
When news from Poitiers was announced to us.
Marie. Words fail to utter how I loathe
that man... Be sure he's at the bottom of
it all.
Countess. Be he, or not, our path of duty's clear, Let us at once away to our
poor friend. *During the last two speeches a gradually increasing noise is heard
at a distance. The* Count *goes to the
window. Count.* Another gathering in
the market-place! These aQitated
groups portend no good;
But in their show are like the pond'rous clouds,
Which send their fatal flashes to the earth.
(Noise increases.)
As I live the strife hegins! The glitter
Of bare swords. Great God! a woman falls,
And with an infant on her breast! A gun!
And others! Oh! Heaven knows where
this will end.
*Corresponding noises in the distance
are heard during*
the Count's *description. The Ladies
rushing up*
to him. The Abbk Raimond *enters in an
excited manner. The* Count *meets him,
leaving*
the Ladies at the Windoio.
Abbe. Dear Count! I come a messenger
of *peace,*
And of *protection,* too, if I may judge
My erring and discordant fellow men.
Fain would I think that all I've seen and heard
Were but the dream of a perturbed brain;
But oh! the infuriate mob!
_A wounded Huguenot *rushes in and
falls down at the* Abbe's *feet. Huguenot.*
Help! help! I die. *Dies.* _The Huguenot
is followed by several Catholics armed
with swords, knives, etc., crying " down
with the Huguenots." Abbe.* Stay, stay,
I charge you; stay your bloody What

means this savage, this infuriate strife?
hands: What plea...what pretext have
you for your rage? Whose orders move
you to this depth of sin?
Catholics (interrupting him). For God
and the King.
Abbe. Who dares speak of God?
Is it His will, think you, that man and man
Should grasp each other's throats in
deadly hate,
And redden the fair earth with human gore,
Because they bend the knee at different shrines?
Though give they utterance to the self-same prayer.
(More shrieks heard.)
Hear ye those shrieks and yet tremble not, lest
That Diety, whose name you now invoke,
Should hurl his thunders on your impious heads,
And crush you in your bloody revelry?
Nay, stand not thus, with bold defiant mien,
But go, and think how best ye may appease
That God whose image here you have destroyed;
And tremble lest the dead man's soul assert
The privilege that you have given it.
The Catholics retreat slowly and defiantly.

Tableau. ACT III.
SCENE I.
SALLE DES PAS PERDUS, PALAIS DE JUSTICE, POITIERS.
27(e *two gaolers,* Jean Baptiste *and* Andre, *playing at dominoes. Jean.* Sapristi!
This Sieur Lomagne is in truth
A fine fellow! But how he frets and fumes
At being inveigled here! And how he has
Escaped the questioning without the rack
Is more than I can rightly understand.
Andre. Poor fellow! So entrapped, he does take on;
And winces, too, as if upon the wheel.
I would not be the man who had decoyed him,

Were he let loose upon me to avenge
The dastard cheat.
Jean. Pristi! Now that's the kind
Of man I feel for. He's none of your poor
Snivelling white-liver'd canaille ;—no,
Nor is he a vain swaggerer either;
For he is just as gentle as a lamb,
And as polite to me,—Jean Baptiste,
First gaoler in the Palais de Justice,—
As if I were the first judge. Nor is he
One of your *grand seigneurs,* who condescends
To extend one single finger to you;
As if the others might be polluted
By your touch. Ah!...Fve always observed
That these are *scurvy knaves;* the veriest
Poltroons when once caged here. Pristi i This is
A rare school wherein to scan our fellow men.
Andre. Ay, that it is, I warrant you.
Some meet
Adversity like *men;* others are *sad,*
Sad cowards. We *do* see some of all sorts.
Jean. Sapristi! Now when I meet these
haughty Ones, I do feel sometimes
churlish; and clang My keys to chafe
their pride. B...r...r...r and make them
That 1—Jean Baptiste—here Ho rule
the roast. feel *Andre.* Not so, Monsieur
Jean Baptiste—for see
I've beat you once again; and I've the
upper hand.
Jean (abstractedly and with pathos).
Sometimes, though, when I'm morose,
my conscience
Tells me I misuse my trust. God only knows
What lurks within the breasts of prisoners;
And oft, methinks, they need the softest words
That we can give them.
Enter Countess *and* Marguerite. *Countess.* Pray tell me, friend, art thou the
gaoler here?
Jean. Ay, Madam—such is indeed my
calling. *Countess.* Will you admit us to
a gentleman
Named Lomagne...a prisoner here...
alas!
Jean. Fain would I, Madam; but I may

not do so
Without a special permit from the Mayor.
Until to-day the Mayor himself could not
Have helped you; for Monsieur Lomagne has been
Under question of the Inquisition.
Marg. But not tortured? Oh! tell me he is safe!
And still unhurt.
Jean. Mademoiselle, he has
Escaped the rack. His frank admissions have,
It seems, protected him from that ordeal.
Marg. Thank heaven, that he is so far safe! But, oh! For mercy-sake! lead us the way to him!
Jean. Truly, Mademoiselle, 'tis more than I Dare do. My post here would be forfeited And I dishonoured. *Countess.* Child—let's to the Mayor,
And be ourselves the bearers of our prayer.
Pardon, my friend, the wrong that we have done
In urging aught that is beyond the scope
Of duty. Women, as you know, are apt
To set at naught all rule...all law...and make
The inspiration of their hearts their guide
Where men do calculate.
Exeunt Countess *and* Marguerite. *Jean.*
Poor young lady! This is too good a school
For artifice. Such tearful eyes as her's
Show clearly what is going on within!
Andre! why tears are trickling down my cheeks,
And something have I in my throat that chokes.
(After gulping and wiping his eyes.)
I'll to the prisoner, and bid him prepare
For the reception of these fair ladies.
Exit.
SCENE II.
PRISON IN THE PALAIS DE JUSTICE. GASPAR. *Gaspar.* How readily is man beguiled by love,
And woman's suasion! The sea was open
To me to have tarried on in safety,
And bid defiance to th' assassin's snare;

But true the proverb is—" God first dements
Whom he would sacrifice!" I seem but as
The shadow of myself; and such is man
When evil overtakes him!
Enter Jean Baptiste. *Jean.* The ladies, sir, of whom I just now told you. *Exit* Jean. *Enter* Countess *and* Marguerite.—
Marguerite *rushes up to* Gaspar, *who retreats. Marg.* Gaspar! dear Gaspar! You *shun* me! Nay Not thus in painful mystery! Speak...speak... stand 1 beseech you speak...what means your chiding?
Gaspar. Oh! Marguerite, what fatal art hast thou
Employed to lure me to this doom? What fiend
Has breathed a poison in your heart? Or is
It priestly machination? To rob me
Of your true love, and crush my fondest hopes...
My faithless dreams?
Marg. Great God! what means this charge?
How have I sinned? what done—to merit this?
Gaspar (taking a letter from his pocket).
Know you this *Marg. (examining it).*
Yes...I sent it you letter? To La Rochelle. *Gasp.* I feared as much.
Marg. Feared? *Gasp.* In cruel mockery of my fall—it was
The only solace left me to reflect on
In my durance. Judge how it solaced when
"Within my cell, in secret prisonment,
No news cams to me from the outer world;
And silence—terrible as that within
The tomb—encompassed me from day to day.
Thinking of thee for whom alone I lived,
I saw thee cold, and passionless, as the
Marble of a lovely statue...nay, worse;
Worse...for by that letter thou hast woven
A web, which holds me, like a poor insect,
In its toils.
Marg. Aunt! Gaspar! Heaven! Do I dream?
(Advances and touches him.)

No...all is too, too, real. What have I done
To be thus tortured?
Countess. My child! My child!
Some mystery is here which needs explaining.
Be calm.
Marg. Oh, aunt! How friendless should I be
Without your heed.—Your loving care.
—'Tis hard
To lack the guidance of a mother's love,
But you fill up the measure of my want;
Give me your counsel in my deep distress.
It is—I know it is—a strain of sense
That raises in him some unworthy doubt.
Gasp. That letter brought me, ''gainst my better sense
To this stronghold of the inquisition,
Whither...by it...my coming was foreseen.
O'er it, I've mused upon the cruel wrong
That's done me, and by one in whom my love,
My fondest.hopes, are centred. Have I not.
Much cause, here, in my lonesome cell, to pray
For that unconscious sleep which laps me in
Forgetfulnes.
Marg. Oh, Gaspar! Gaspar!
Reproach in words which sound so like to love,
Is tenfold insupportable. I see
    Tlicu coldly doubtest still. That letter was
Indited by the counsel of our friend
The Governor of Auvergue.—I bound it
To the arm of one who was commended
To me as a trustworthy messenger,
And bade him hasten with it to llochelle.
Gasp. And from his arm 1 took it; I followed
Its direction; repaired to the Hotel
De France, and found myself a prisoner.
Marg. The Hotel de France! Never have I heard
Of such a place in Poitiers; *looking at the letter)* and yet
Here expressed! There must be some

bewitchment His
Wherein, alas! I fear me much, I am
The cause, and you the unhappy victim.
Gasp. Are we the sport of foul bedevil-
ment?
Demons—they say—do sometimes lay
their hold
On forms the fairest; and in sinless
breasts
Take their abode,—to consummate a
vile
And fiendish purpose; until, exorcised
By some pious rite, they are expelled
Their beauteous lodgment.
Marg. Oh! wretched fate.
My eye-balls throb; but have no tears
to shed.
You do not think me faithless Gaspar?
No!
Oh! say but no. For sure the very
thought,
The shadow of a doubt will drive me
mad.
Heaven knows! my every thought, my
prayers are thine.
Gasp. No, dearest, *no.* Though by some
magic spell
The forced avowal comes from thine
own lips
In spite of *this,* the writing of your hand,
I'll think you true—true as the finest
steel.
Forgive my doubt; and oh! my Mar-
guerite dear,
Let me but look upon your lovely face,
And I will think of naught but rapturous
love—
Love—which in fancy I have oft pro-
longed
Into another and a future life,
When I have had you in my fond em-
brace
As I have now; and held your silky head
Upon my breast. Then—then all earthly
things
Were tinged with heaven. Give me
again the glance
Of those uplifted eyes, and I'll forget
My woes, and think this cell a paradise.
Marg. My life! my love!.
Enter Jean Baptiste. *Jean.* Your pardon,
ladies—but the accorded hour Has
passed. *Countess.* Is't possible? And
hold you to The very letter of the grant
allowed us? *Jean.* Madam, willingly

would I prolong the time; But my instructions are for one hour only. *Marg.*
Think of the best, the dearest friend
thou hast, And judge what thou wouldst
feel wert thou as I am! *Jean.* All that
you say I feel, fair lady, and Never
thought that I could be so tempted.
Marg. Gaspar! *(sobbing.) Gasp.* Go,
dearest, go! Better to yield,
As now perforce we must, than risk the
blest,
Th enchanting prospect of another
meeting.
Like a bright star, thy presence here lias
made
These gloomy walls seem radiant; and
joy
Keturns where all before was bitterness.
Leading Margueuite *sobbing to the
door. Exeunt*
Countess *taking leave, and* Marguerite.
*Door
closes.*
Again no sound! Yet have I solace
now
To while away the tardy hours which,
erst,
Like those before the dawn, appeared
most dark.
So mingled are the bitters and the
sweets
In the world's course, that everything
conspires
To show how little this life has to
give,
And death how little has to take
away.
Why cherish we then life, or fear we
death?
SCENE III. ROOM IN COUNT DE LANOYS'
HOTEL AT POITIERS.
M. De Montmerin, Count *and* Countess
De Lanoys, *and* Marie. *Count.* Maitre
Laroche, I hear, is a good man,
And also a distinguish'd advocate.
Neither will he barter his own honour,
Nor that of any client he may have.
Our friend, knowing no one here, de-
pends on us
To find him skilful and experienced
counsel.
Expecting you, 1 have requested him
To pass this way; and we may look
for him.
Mont. 'Tis that which brings me here. I

am informed That he is no longer under secret Questioning; also that his advocate May now have unrestrained ac-
cess to him. But I've a galliard caged,
who may require A brief visit from your
niece and daughter, Whose tale—if I
mistake not—may avail Our friend as
much as any advocate. Know you
Maitre Laroche? *Count.* Not exactly,
But I have vouchers recommending
him.
Marie (apart to Countess).
"*A galliard whose tale may avail our
friend
As much as any advocate!*" What can
He mean?
Countess. Possibly he has discovered
Some clue to the mysterious bearing
Of poor Gaspar. I'm sure I hope he has.
Enter Servant *followed by* Maitre
Laroche. *Servt.* Monsieur Laroche. *Exit*
Servant. *Count.* I thank you much, sir,
for this timely visit;
For we have an affair which gives us
great
Disquiet. A prisoner here in Poitiers,
Whose case we wish to relegate to you.
Laroche. I've heard as much, and, from
my heart, Desire to render you effective
service. should know *Countess.* Me-
thinks, good sir, 'twere right that you
That he in whom we are so much con-
cerned Is of the new religion, like our-
selves. *Laroche.* Madam, I'm not the
less disposed to stand by him. *Marie.*
It's no light matter you will have in
hand, But you will save him? *Laroche.*
Be sure I'll do my best.
But let us look on all things as they are.
It is not by the heart, but by the head
That we must con the situation o'er,
And in it bow to this—that he's a man
And will by men be tried.
Marie. "lis just in that
I ground my strongest hope. Women,
you know,
Are guided by their hearts, and by their
hearts
Made headstrong. Man's citadel is dou-
bly weak:
For he may be assail'd through heart
and head.
And is it not a glorious privilege,
To lead your fellow men by words—
mere words?

Larocho. But in an unjust cause, words surely fail,

When conscience fails to furnish reasoning.

Marie. Ay! but his cause *is* just; and yet begirt

With just so much of tenet, that conscience

Might obtrude itself, to blind man's reason.

Not yours, I know.

Countess (to Laroche). I humbly pray you, sir,

Pardon the zeal of her enthusiasm.

The blow, we are assured, is dealt by some

Perfidious hand, moved by the tiger's wrath,

But guided by the cunning of the fox.

Laroche. 1 know...I kuow...But I would first confer

With the pris'ner; and with iiim organise

Our system of defence; that being done I will return to you.

Mont. In the meantime

He may not know the sum of all that's charg'd

Against him. But a copy of the notes

Will be placed at your service by the Judge

Of Instruction, for your better guidance.

Laroche. By such concession shall I profit much;

And grateful am 1 for the privilege. *Exit.*

Countess. Now that all human wit is set to work,

Yet one thing more, methinks, 'twere well to do.

There is a shrine hard by, of sovereign power,

The tomb which once contained St. Radigonde;

To this the sick repair for their relief,

And ill-starred men for turn of fortune's wheel.

Let us to it for a prosperous issue,

The spell is one of hallowed sanctity.

Count. E'en as you will, my wife, your faith is great,

And, as your saying is, such trust does spread. you. *Mont.* I have heard of that same shrine, and I will with *Marie.*

Shall I impart to Marguerite where we

go? *Countess.* She's best alone; for much she needs repose.

Exeunt.

Marguerite *enters, finding the room empty. Marg.* All gone! And yet why not? for sure 'tis right That I the solitude, which bears him down, Should also feel. *Going to the window.*

But whither go my friends? Doubtless, for me, on some kind errand bent!

(Turning round she sees De Courtines, *who has*

stealthily followed her in.)

What may this mean? How found you entrance here?

Wherefore, I pray, this ill-timed intrusion?

Court. What if my purpose be to offer help?

For such 1 know you need; and I have here

Retainers, fain and ripe to do my charge.

Art willing to revoke thy taunts and gibes,

And, for the doomed life—that I may save—

Thyself, in quittance, give into my arms?

Marg. Art thou a man? And can'st thou, unabash'd,

Give utterance to so foul and vile a compact?

Too infamous for darkness to conceal.

Court. You cavil at the terms! Yet one word more— Nothing impossible have I devised— This very night my serfs can set him free, And bear him whither he may choose to go For safety. If thou wilt away with me. *Marg.* Away with thee! What devil haunts thy soul, To make thy thoughts as loathsome as thyself? *Court.* To the winds all pitiful forbearance!

And hearken now to what is not a dream.

The scaffold whereupon thine idol dies

Is now prepared. The faggots are upheaped,

The manacles are clenched into the stake,

To pinion and restrain his writhing limbs,

As curling flames surround and lick their prey.

(marguerite *shrieks.)*

The picture fascinates! Imperious dame!

Marg. Serpent! For thou art neither more nor less— Draw back into thy slimy mouth that tongue Whose fork'd flickering holds its victim spell-bound. Gloat as thou may'st o'er anguish in thy toils, I spurn both thee and thine accursed nature. *Court.* You drive me then to force?—Well, be it so— I have my minions at my beck and call, And I will use them to convey you hence, In such a litter as befits your state. Rave as you may, your cries will only pass For those of one possess'd. A little time In wholesome solitude may change your mind. *During this speech* Marguerite *mores almost imperceptibly to a side of the room where daggers, fyc, are suspended to the wall. Court.* What, ho! *Whistles, at the same time* Marguerite *calls. Marg.* Help! Help! 2nd Emissary *rushes in at one door and* Gabrielle *at another. During this time* Marguerite *seizes one of the daggers. Court.* Seize her, and bear her to the litter. gabrielle *throws herself between the* Emissary *and* Marguerite; *the latter recognising the* Emissary, *addresses* De Courtines.

Marg. A fit companion that, for men like thee!

Approach one step, or give one other sign,

And in my heart this dagger will I sheath.

My blood upon thine head.

de Courtines *making a step in advance, but as if*

to speak, Marguerite *points the dagger to her*

heart, when approaching steps are heard. De

Courtines *and* Emissary *retire quickly as*

curtain falls.

ACT IV.

SCENE I.

SAME SCENE AS LAST.

(M. DE MONTMERIN, CoTJNT DE IjANOYS, MARGUERITE,

and Marie.) *Laroche.* The more I study him the more I see

That he's the victim of his dauntless

heart.
'Tis true, the torture may have wrung from him
What he has freely owned; but, as I learn,
The first and foremost charge against him sworn
Is disaffection to the King and State;
And 'gainst that impeachment we've an answer.
Mont. But for the declaration of his faith,
Then, his case is hopeful?
Laroche. Ay more; for by
The changeful version of the massacre,
Each wavering plea confutes the others,
And judgment needs must halt.
Marie. It *is* then

More to the heart than to the head that siege Three different pleas were urged by Chnrles in vindication of the massacre of St. Bartholomew: first, the well-known feud between Coligny and the Guises, for which latter Charles asserted that the zeal of the people could not be restrained, and hence the massacre. But the Due de Guise, it seems, had sufficient power to compel the king to retract that attempt at vindication. The second plea was that given to the Earl of Worcester—an envoy from Elizabeth—namely, that a Huguenot conspiracy had been formed, with no less a man than the Admiral Coligny at its head; but this was obviously a fabrication, as all the antecedents of Coligny proved. The third plea was that the Huguenots themselves were the cause of the massacre, by placing Charles under the necessity of making war with Spain, and that the king, by the advice of Tavenner, chose that course which he thought least prejudicial, and as salutary to the Catholic religion as it appeared to be to the State.

Must now be laid! But I'm prepared for both.

And, like a skilful general, hold a force

Reserv'd to carry every intrenchment.

What if you have a helpmate in the cause,

To assail the heart, whilst ycu make all things clear

To reason?
Laroche (jokingly). Methinks 'twould go hard with us If we did not prosper.
Count. "What means the child?
Some further spell, I trow, of magic power—
Another Radigonde?
Marie. Nothing, alas!

So superhuman. But an if tlie source
By which he was entrapp'd, were made to serve
For his acquittance?
Laroche (seriously). Pray explain yourself.
Marg. May I explain? We've conn'd the project o'er, And fain I would that you a colleague had, To take a step where you might fear to tread. *Laroche.* You doubt, then, my ability? *Marg.* No...no.
But were you join'd with one who'd emulate
Your zeal, yet not as rival; who'd cope witli you,
Yet not in competition; who would serve
Your cause, yet be no confrere. Say, would you
Scorn such aid?
Laroche. E'en then, my oath, and duty
To my calling *might* forbid th' assistance.
Marg. And you would see a man with quiet conscience
Mount the scaffold, when duty set at naught
Would save him? Great God! what strange thoughts men
Of duty!...But were / your adjutant? have
(Love's fertile in strategy.)...Words failing
You—my soul, methinks, would find expression
In such showing, that words could never breathe.
Laroche. Curtail'd of all affection, a judge's heart
Admits *stern facts,* but with Draconian will
Abjures all *sentiment.* I fear me much
The generous sparks that you would fan into
A fire, will find no biding place, where most
We need it.

Marg. No human heart so hard but it will bend
To some emotion. Why then yield the license
Of my sex, and reason like as men do?
God speaks in various ways, and none more suasive,
Though *devoid* of *reason,* than th' impulsive
Language of the soul...Oh! let me ply it:
For therein have I faith that mocks possession.
Laroche. Be it as you will. But how will you appear?
Marg. I'll ape no outward garb to seem like you;
For I have that within me which will well
Repay your generous aid, and vindicate
A maiden's waywardness.
Laroche. It's a brave will
That you have summoned to your passing need!
And nothing do I ken to bar the trial.
I will stand by, and may God speed you in it!

SCENE II.

COURT IN THE PALAIS DE JUSTICE. *Three judges, with spectators. On one side of them* Montmerin, *and on the other* Count De Lanoys. Marguerite *and* Marie *on* right. Maitre Laroche *on the left.* Crier *in front.* Crier. The Court! *Enter* Gaspar, *introduced by* Jean Baptiste, *on left.* De Courtines *and* Karl Fritz *on right.* President (to Gaspar). Prisoner, stand forth and hear the exposition of the facts of which you are accused. You have been examined in the "Sanctum Officium," and declared to be " Hereticus perseverans in errore." His Majesty the King, however, not tolerating an ecclesiastical tribunal which would encroach upon his own sovereign authority, has transferred you now to this our secular Court. We are not, therefore, the mere executors of the episcopal verdict, but declare to you other charges wherewith you are accused, and the names of your accusers, that you may answer all. The crime of heresy you have admitted in confessing to have adopted the tenets of the reformed religion; and it now remains to examine you on the charge of disaffection to His very High and Powerful Majesty the King and to the State, of which you stand accused by Henri de Courtines. How say you to this accusation? *Gaspar.* You teach me, sirs, what auswer I should give, By your summing up of the impeachment Which is preferred against me. True it is That I am what is called a Huguenot, For which I'm sentenced by the bloody ritual Of an alien Inquisition to the stake. Such is the custom, but I know no law To sanction judgment ruled by foreign Court, Under the pretext of religious test; May it not be that feudal policy Takes more account of its own peril than The extinction of a creed? But think not That I vindicate my faith on such a plea, Nor judge the perturbation of my soul To servile fear of death. I've faced it oft, And in so many ways, that base it is, And cowardly—I ween—to quail before it. There's not a night but that we seek to lose The consciousness which we so fear to lose When death o'ertakes us. But the apprehension Of the waking may well intimidate The stoutest heart; and therein 'tis I'll stake My tenets against yours, and welcome death In the venture. But on the other score Of disaffection to the State, I pray you Put me to the question; and if in aught I've proved myself a traitor, I stand accursed, And the very *recreants* who have brought Me hither...ay, even *they*...might loathe me And pass on...Then would the death you send me to Be fraught, indeed, with terror; for it would Taint me with dishonour; and in face of *that* I own myself a coward. But you will not, You cannot show one act, one word of mine That will make good the charge of disaffection. *President:* Henri de Courtines—stand forth and attest The special charges you've already sworn to. *Court.* You were in league with Henri, Prince de Conde, When, aiming at the Crown, he coined false money Bearing his effigy, and his own name As King of France impress'd upon each piece. *Gaspar.* That was a base artifice; but by whom Concocted I know not. Clearly it aimed At nothing but the downfall of the

Prince, And punishment was threatened by Coliguy To any who should circulate the coin. *Court.* You were associated with Coliguy When, following on the battle of Jarnac, He advocated an appeal to arms. *Caspar.* "Pis false. When Admiral Coligny heard That at a secret council 'twas resolved To bring him to the stake, he counsel'd peace And vow'd that rather than a war provoke, And its attendant horrors, he'd be dragged, A lifeless corse, through every street in Paris. *Court.* You 'scaped from Paris at the very time When you were being intrusted with a charge To Prince Louis of Nassau, in Holland. *Gaspar.* No proposition had been made to me. Simply was I told that I'd been named As a fit person for that same mission; But I had seen a letter from the Pope Indited to the Cardinal of Lorraine, Which noted treachery to the Huguenots In Paris, and I therefore left the place. *(After a pause* Laroche *rises to address the Court.) Laroche.* The subtle charges, sirs, which we have heard, Conjoined with the decree of heresy, To make the *show* of truth appear more true, Have—each and all—been proved fallacious. It is not, therefore, mercy that I ask. But simply justice for the prisoner. The verdict of the Inquisition must Perforce be false; else must the State be false In granting *that* for which he is made guilty. The practice of the new religion is Allowed by treat', and four towns are held As pledges of good faith. The observance Of that doctrine is therefore justified; But priestly craft says *no;* and by such plea Justice is silenced. But we are also told

That kingly power is power ordain'd by God, And disobedience to that power is true Rebellion against God, who first 'stablished And maintains it. Which then, I ask, is wrong? The prisoner who reveres the sovereign compact, Or the prelate who would violate it? Such an encroachment on the Right Divine *Is—must be*—unduteous; and a sovereign's Acquiescence in such arrogance *wrong.* Sirs, we're also told that there's a limit Where obedience *ceases* as a duty; And that if public good be best promoted By resisting wrong, then is rebellion Justified, and lays claim to right divine As truly as the greatest potentate. But loyalty scorns boasting;—hence no need Is there to swell the truth of each reply That has been made so undeniable. It may be, though, that you will take into Account the circumstance by which capture Was effected; and in your judgment make Expressive shipwreck of the perfidy. *(The* JUdges *confer together.) President.* Prisoner! Standing as you now may be Upon the brink of that dread gulph which none Can e'er repass, I charge you speak, if you Have aught to urge, which may, perchance, avail Against our sentence—ere it be too late. *Gasp.* Nothing have I to say more than I've said. *Marg.* Oh! pause—I pray you pause, and let me speak. It was, you know, by foul and treacherous Semblance of my writing that you have now To hold the trembling scales 'twixt life and death. By my soul's suit, in mercy let me speak. *(A pause whilst the* Judges *confer.) President.* Lady! The Court consents, though the Be strange, to grant your supplication. request It will

allow you a patient hearing To all that you may have to say. Proceed. *Marg.* You said *too late* I Oh heaven! what means *too* In your interpretation of the law *late?* May not some fault, some flaw, by chance intrude? And so set forth a claim to further search? It *is not* then...it *cannot* be too late To cancel a death judgment. What if life Be forfeited to erring *prejudice?* And not to equity? What if the scales Be equal in their poise, and need but *mercy* To decide their turn? Remorse will not correct The faulty balance; nor will the crime be less, Regret it as you may, if e'er your conscience Should reproach you for that lack of *mercy.* A sentence may be reconsidered, Not so a life that's forfeited. Pause, then, And give an ear to my appeal for *mercy.* When raek'd with pain, or pillow'd in the joy Of buoyant health, who has not felt the balm Of an approving sense of some kind act,— Some tender word,—some blessed deed of *mercy?* And will you rob yourselves of so much bliss When dwelling on the memory of the past? Or tempt your God to turn a senseless ear To fervent prayers of yours? Oh! be *merciful!* Which of you is so lonely in the world That he has not a friend,—a wife,—or child,— Perhaps a lover,—in whose faithful breast Your every hope in life is firmly moored; For whom you'd sacrifice your all—yourself— Without a thought or hope of a return? (*Taking the hand of* Gaspar.)
Such is this man to me. For him I crave, By all that's dear to you, your tender *mercy.*
I love him with an entire devotion;
Such as, methinks, was never felt before.
When nature framed him for her masterpiece,
No other could she than to shape him as
A mark for every euvious shaft—and one,
Alas! has struck him. But you'll have *mercy!*
And vindicate the God-like attribute
That man acquires, when, clothed in special power,
He shows most *mercy.* (judges *confer* and look impatient.)
More would I urge; but by your downcast looks,
And threatening brows 1 am oppressed.
Yet bear with me, and I doubt not to fiud
In each of you a good man's sympathy.
(After a short pause.)
I'm told there is an ancient form of trial
Which virtue honours and which knavery shuns,
For judgment comes from One who never errs.
Were I the prisoner I would cast my fate
Into the scale where dwells that Arbiter,
And ask this man *(taking* Gaspar's *hand again)* to be my
So boundless is my faith in his stout heart. champion,
And in his prowess! I will silence fear,
And urge him to the ordeal by combat.
Laroche. How grand! How perfectly divine is woman! *Whilst* Laroche *is speaking* Marguerite *staggers and falls fainting. The* Count, Marie, *and* Gaspar *rush up to her and raise her to a seat.*
Marg. A moment's faintness—but 'tis over now.
What have I said? What done in my dismay,
To steel myself against my woman's nature?
Gasp. My guardian angel! My soul's own idol!
I've heard that gems possess'd of magic power
Change in their colour as their spell proceeds;
And now I see your ruby lips regain
Their innate hue,—their charm accomplished.
(Turning to the Judges.)
As I am admonished, haply the Court Will so accord to me my noble birthright—
The privilege of battle. In this cause
I say and do affirm, that every charge
Proposed and urged against me by that cur
Is false as hell;—and this I do declare
That he's a miscreant, and a liar;
The truth whereof I'm ready to maintain
With hazard of my life and dearest blood.
(The Judges *confer)*
President. Henri de Courtines——If the revealment
Made by this intriguing emissary
Be truthful, you cannot be innocent.
And in such case the Court requires of you
To take the part as anciently hath been
According to the custom and the law
At arms.
Court. You take me somewhat by surprise!
Gasp. Not quite so much as you'd have done by me, Nor as the law would now observe to you Failing this chance to save you from its clutch. *Court.* How know you all is true that you have heard Imputed to me by this scurvy knave? *(To the* Judges, *referring to* Karl.) *Gasp.* That base and treacherous object would disgrace The solace of revenge. *(To Court.)* My bout's with you. The hatching of your plot was overheard, And by no willing ears. You schemed a course— A hellish course, with fiend-like assassins, For my murder; and 1 take advantage Of the turn to avenge it. But between *Valiant* men *(ironically)* the venture should be equal, And now I call upon you to redeem Your nature, if such can be. There's my gage. *(Throwing down a glove.) Court.* I have no relish for such tournament. *Gasp.* You shrink not to avoid the path of honour; But fail to see that, having so transgress'd, Life is not worth the holding. *Base coward!* you. *Court.* I'll not endure your taunts, nor crouch before *(Taking up the gage.)* To whatsoever the Court enjoins I'm bound. *President.* What surety do you bring that you'll observe The form and usage of judicial combat? *Court.* The word and honour of a gentleman,
I stake as surety of such observance.
President. Gaspar Lomagne demands the privilege
Of battle in proof of his innocence;
And Henri de Courtines accepts the pledge.

"We, as vicegerents to His Majesty,
And in the arbitrement of our right,
Do hereby admit you to a duel,
In the presence of our Court assembled;
And assign to'you the third day from this
From the fourth hour until it be starlight.
And we enjoin you, there and then, to do
And perform your parts to your utmost power.
If the defendant was able to persist in the combat till starlight be was acquitted. ACT V.
SCENE I.
THE TILT-YARD ADJOINING THE PALAIS DE JUSTICE. *A centre seat slightly elevated for the Judges. Seats on each side for spectators. On one side a Gallows with a halter hanging from it; the custom being that when the defendant on trial by combat was worsted and not killed he was immediately hanged. Enter* Francois *and* Jean Baptiste. *Francois.* It seems to me that a good cudgelling
Would as corrective be as any wound
Inflicted by these ugly swords; and if
I had the use of the batons, I'd do
His business for him; by the holy mass
He should not soon forget th' experiment.
Jean. But there's some glitter in the swords. Pristi!
And glitter—after all—men dearly love.
It's a vain world! and trifles, light as air,
Graft such opinions on the base-born mind,
As nobles feed on, though they scorn the lout
That fosters them. There would be no tall man
Were there not one that's shorter; nor your noble
Without the serf, 'gainst whom he views himself,
Although, in merit, the serf be peerless.
And so the world wags on! Your nobleman
Must fight with *swords;* bondsmen with truncheons.
Francois. You're a ripe scholar, Master Jean Baptiste! Where learnt you all these morals? *Jean.* In my work.

Sapristi! a gaoler's life is thoughtful;
And I've much yielded to that mood of life:
It makes one cynical perhaps; for ne'er
Saw I the man whose inward bent could bear
It's full revealment to the light of day.
Now, there's your hero of to-day! Why, he
Is just as proud as Lucifer himself!
But hoodwinks you by affability
(Good-fellowship 'tis called by hangers on,
But give me spendthrifts for good-fellowship!)
Yet better meek than lordly arrogance,
Which his antagonist is given too,
And he's a sad poltroon, I trow. Pristi!
All men are so when swollen with vanity.
But see the judges come—I must away
To bring these doughty combatants together.
Enter Judges, *followed by* Montmerin, *who conducts* Marguerite, *the* Count *conducting* Marie.
The ladies are placed together on one side. The
President *and* Judges *take their seats in the*
centre.
President. Let the appellant enter first the lists.
caspar *is introduced by* Jean Baptiste.
Lomagne, you swear that by no spell, no herb,
No witchcraft, nor by demoniac aid,
Your sword bears an enchantment, nor your arm
A cabalistic power, trothless in duel.
Gasp. I swear; and pledge my honour to conform
To every rule enjoin'd in single combat.
President. Bring forth the appellee into the lists.
courtines *is conducted in on opposite side by* Andre.
Courtines, you swear that by no charm, no spell,
No practised sorcery, your arm and sword
Have potency beyond good faith and truth.
Court. I swear. But first I'd urge this

counterplea,
That the defendant is a Heretic,
And, as such, disentitled to his claim.
The privilege of judicial combat.
President. But trial, such as this, though disallow'd
In matters appertaining to the Court
Presided over by Hierophants,
Is oft demanded and admitted here.
Your counterplea, then, is beside the mark;
And, as it seems to us, no other course
Is left you but the pursuit of the gage,
Or, failing, brand yourself a recreant.
After a short pause. It now remains to publish the three banns Ordain'd for the inception of a duel. Let them be now proclaim'd; then to the strife. *Jean.* 1st. No blood-relations of the combatants May be present. If any such be here They are commanded to retire forthwith. 2nd. The utmost silence is required. And last, 3rd. Above all things it is prohibited To give assistance or by word or deed. *To be read. President (throwing the gage into the arena).* Proceed. gaspar *and* Couktines *now confront each other, and after*
some fencifig, Gaspar *disarms* Couktines.
Gasp. Take up your sword, and try to be more cautious
In the use of it. Henceforth no quarter.
courtines *takes up his sword, and, by the resolute*
bearing of Gaspar, *is made to resume the combat,*
when he is mortally wounded, and falls.
Court. I'm hit! Oh! sir, forgive me, if in aught I've sinned against you—as I fear I have. Swell not the measure of my guilty course; But ob! In tender mercy speak of me When I am gone...for now...too late...I feel... The pang of deep remorse...and fain would staunch This flowing blood...to rescue...from the grasp... Of death...my faltering heart... too late...your hand... All's dark dark *Dies. Gasp.* (to Judges) Have I uprightly done my duty here? *President.* Most rightfully, and I pronounce thee free. The arms and body of thine adversary Are thine to have and deal with as thou wilt. *Gasp. (going to the body and*

standing over it). Dead! and how changed in one brief minute's span! That face—but now the index of a mind Within, is blank and inexpressive.

The vaporous atoms of the blood, which coursed

The veins and centered in the heart, are now

Diffused, and give expression to the sun's bright beam.

And *so* the soul expands into another world!

I do repent me now that I have warr'd

With this poor piece of earth, here lying

At my feet...'Tis passing wonderful How death extinguishes resentment! *(Advancing to the* President.) From heaven I gain'd the strength to vanquish him, And heaven, I trust, will give him full atonement. I would not add one gibe to his defeat; But with all reverence commend his corse To decorous and respectful obsequies. *All the spectators advance in front of the body so as to form a screen before it. The* Count *and* Mont-Merin *advance, conducting* Marguerite *between them.* Montmerin *presents* Marguerite *to* Gaspak.

Mont. What more befitting now than the reward

Which thou hast nobly won? the place, 'tis true,

Is not in harmony with dulcet sounds; But where discord yields the palm to fondness,

No time nor place, methinks, can be unsuited.

Gasp. Beloved Marguerite, thy presence here

Made Heaven seem smiling on my rightful cause,

And gave the mettle you relied upon. Judge then the recognition I should feel For my own life, and more than life, in thee!

Marg. I'm proud, Fm very proud to hear thy lips

Approve of my resource in desperation.

But, if recognition be expressed by love, I fear me, 1 shall be a boundless usurer. *Gasp.* I'm rich in that, and any score can pay.

But we have yet another arbiter In this indulgent mimic world to sway. Wilt thou still hold the license of thy sex,

And set forth a claim for its approval? *Marg.* That will I, for I see no downcast looks, Nor threatening brows to daunt my showing. *(To the audience.)*
I may dispense with law—so says my brief—

But lest my woman's pleading come to grief,

If any here there be who do no wrong, A horsehair wig and silken gown to don;

To your forensic prowess I appeal, To bring—without demur—that genial zeal

To bear upon the end we have in view—

Your approbation. Praise gilds all things new.

Plaudits—you   know—we   actors dearly love.

From Pit and Boxes, and from Gods above.

PRINTED BY EFFINGHAM WILSON, ROYAL EXCHANGE. COMMERCIAL AND OTHER WORKS PUBLISHED AND SOLD BY EFFINGHAM WILSON, gjsblxsjpr, iprinta, *§aak&dkt,* §ittbtr, fngrafar, *mis* Stationer,

11, ROYAL EXCHANGE, LONDON.
TO WHICH IS ADDED A LIST OF VALUABLE BOOKS of REFERENCE essential to COMMERCIAL ESTABLISHMENTS and PUBLIC COMPANIES.
GUIDE BOOKS for TRAVELLERS, Sc., &c. In addition to the Works enumerated in this Catalogue, The Books or All Othek Publishers may be had at this Establishment immediately on their Publication.

Tate's Modern Cambist.
A MANUAL OF FOREIGN EXCHANGES.
The Modern Cambist: forming a Mannal of Foreign Exchanges in the various operations of Bills of Exchange and Bullion, according to the practice of ail Trading Nations; with Tables of Foreign Weights and Measures, and their Equivalents in English and French. By

William Tate, Principal of the City of London   Commercial   Educational Establishment. "A work of great excellence. The care which has rendered this a standard work is still exercised, to cause it to keep pace, from time to time, with the changes in the monetary system of foreign nations."—*The Times.*
"Constitutes a work which deserves the high reputation it has justly acquired, both here and on the Continent, as a 'standard authority' with the mercantile world." —*Daily News.*

Sixteentli Edition, Enlarged and Rewritten. Price 12. « 1
October, 1876.
4 LONDON! EFFINGHAM WILSON, KOYAL EXCHANGE.
Robinson's Share and Stock Tables;

Comprising a set of Tables for Calculating the Cost of any number of Shares, at any price from l-16th of a pound sterling, or *Is.* 3d. per share, to £310 per share in value; and from 1 to 500 shares, or frcm £100 to £50,000 stock.

"These excellent and elaborate tables will be found exceedingly useful to bankers, public companies, stockbrokers, and all those who have any dealings in shares, bonds, or stocks of any and every description."—*Daily News.* Fifth Edition, price 5i., cloth.

Burgon's Life and Times of Sir Thomas Gresham,

Including notices of many of his contemporaries. By John Wm. Burgon, Esq. Offered at the *reduced price ofQs.* In two handsome large octavo volumes, embellished with a fine Portrait, and twenty-nine other Engravings, *elegantly hound in cloth. Published at* £1 10.

Hoare's Mensuration for the Million;

Or, the Decimal System and its applications to the Daily Employments of the Artisan and Mechanic. By Chakles Hoare.

"This is a painstaking exposition of the many advantages derivable from the use of decimals; we therefore welcome it with all the cordiality due to those who simplify the process of calculation. "—*Practical Mechanic.*

Ninth Thousand. Price Is.
Benedict's (A) Word to My Wife: Practical Hints in Cookery and Com-

fort. By A Benedict.

Fifth Thousand. Price *6d.*

Doubleday's Financial and Monetary History.

A Financial, Monetary, and Statistical History or England, from the Revolution of 1688 to the present time; derived principally from Official Documents. By Thomas Doubleday, Author of 'The True Law of Population,' &c, &c.

"A work of absorbing interest and uncommon research. We have tested it minutelv, and believe it strictly true, as it is unquestionably clear in its statements."—*Blackwood's Edinburgh Magazine.*

In 1 vol., 8vo. Price £2 *is., cloth.* Very scarce.

Clifford's Life Assurer's Handbook and Key to Life Assurance.

Articles on Life Assurance Companies, republished from Articles expressly written for 'The Bullionist.' Edited by George Ciamord, Esq. Price *5s.*

Combe's Currency Question Considered.

"This pamphlet is a service rendered to the commercial public. No such work has hitherto been attainable. Mr. Combe's pamphlet fulfils everything that could be desired, as it is a concise and logical statement, and will save wading through a mass of contradictory treatises. Its broad and simple doctrines leave no excuse for those who may continue to trouble the community with incessant effusions on this matter." —*The Times, March 4th,* 1856.

Eleventh Edition. Price *2s., cloth.*

Crump's Exchange, Yield, and Share Tables,

Calculated especially to meet the requirements of the new system of Currency in Germany. By Aetiiur Chump. Second Edition. Price *0t.* _____

Fox's One Hundred Golden Rules (or Axioms) of Account Keeping.

By An Accountant. Fourth Edition. Price *Q.,* sewed.

Fox's One Hundred Debtor and Creditor Maxims of Account Keeping.

Price 6£, sewed.

Fox's Laws of Book-keeping.

Part I. Single Entry. By an Accoun-

tant. Price *§d.*

Lewis's Tables for finding the Number of Days,

From one day to any other day in the same or the following year. By William Lewis. Price 12s. *6d.*

The Rationale of Market Fluctuations.

By a City Editok. Price *7s. 6d.*

Royle's Laws relating to English and Foreign Funds, Shares and Securities. The Stock Exchange, its Usages, and the Rights of Vendors and Purchasers.

With 400 References to Acts of Parliament and decided cases, and an Analytical Index. By William Boyle, Solicitor. Price 6s.

Walton's Complete Calculator and Universal Ready Reckoner,

For all numbers from 1 to 80,000, at any rate or price, from One Farthing to Twenty Shillings. 8vo. Price £3 3s., cloth. Very Scarce.

i-n 6 LONDON: EFFINGHAM WILSON, KOYAL EXCHANGE.

Booth's Tables of Simple Interest,

On a New Plan of Arrangement; by which the Interest of any number of Pounds, from One to a Thousand, for any number of Days not exceeding a Year, will be found at one view, without the trouble or risk of additions, at any rate per cent. 4to. Price £5 5s. Very Scarce.

Ferguson's Buyers' and Sellers' Guide; or, Profit on Return.

Showing on one view Net Cost and Return Prices, with a Table of Discount. By Andrew Ferguson, Author "of Tables of Profit, Discount, Commission,

and Brokerage.'

Net Profit on Returns.—Price 1., sewed.

Pulbrook's Ballot Act, T872,

With Analytical References, and Copious Index. Pocket Edition. By Anthony Pulbrook, Solicitor. Limp cloth, 126 pp., with 1500 References. Price 2s.

Pulbrook's Treatise on Companies limited by Guarantee;

Showing their Applicability to Mining and other Commercial purposes. By Anthony Pulbrook, Solicitor. Price 2s. 6c?., cloth.

Vincent's Law of Criticism and Li-

bel.

A Handbook for Journalists, Authors, and the Libelled. By C. Howard Vincent. Price 2s. *Gd.*

Wilson's Shilling Diary.

"The cheapest and best diary ever issued to the public."—*Morning Advertiser.* Published Annually, in cloth. Interleaved, with ruled paper. Price Is. *6d.* , cloth.

Pulbrook's Companies' Act, 1862-7; Stannaries' Act, 1869; Life Assurance Companies' Act, 1870, &c,

With Analytical References, a very copious Index, and the Rules in Chancery.

Fourth Edition. By Anthony Pulbrook, Solicitor. Price 6s., cloth.

"Likely to have an extensive circulation. "—*Standard.*

"Best edition published."—*Mining Journal.*

Rutter's Exchange Tables between England, India, and China.

With new Intermediate Rates of thirty seconds of a Penny per Rupee, sixteenths of a Penny per Dollar, and one quarter of a Rupee per Hundred Dollars; also New and Enlarged Tables of Premium and Discount on Dollars, of Bullion, and of indirect Exchanges between England, India, and China. By Henry Rutter, late Agent of the Commercial Bank of India, Hong Kong. New edition. Price £110s., cloth.

Rutter's General Interest Tables

For Dollars, Francs, Milreis, &c, adapted to both the English and Indian Currency, at Rates varying from 1 to 12 per cent., on the Decimal System. By Henry Ruttee. Price 10s. *&d.*

Rutter's Metrical System of Weights and Measures Tables

Compared with the British Standard Weights and Measures in a complete Set of Comparative Tables; also, Tables of Equivalent Prices under the Two Systems, and of Chinese and Indian Weights compared with Metric Weights, &c. By Heney Ruttee. Price 4s., cloth.

Rutter's Silk and Tea Tables.

Price 10s., cloth.

Maertens' Silk Tables,

Showing the cost of Silk per pound,

avoirdupois and kilo, as purchased in *Japan* and laid down in London and Lyons. Price 30s.

Maertens' Silk Tables, *J* ...

Showing the cost of Silk per pound, avoirdupois and kilo, as purchased at *Shanghai* and laid down in London and Lyons. Second Edition. Price 30s.

Wilson's Importance of Punctuality. On Sheet. Price *6d.*

Adam's Tables of Exchange.

Arranged Decimally; exhibiting the Equivalent of any Sum from 1 pie to 100 rupees, or from 1 penny to £100 sterling, in regular gradations at the different rates of exchange, from Is. 9rf. to 2s. *id.* per rupee, ascending by T'5 of a penny. By Geoege Uee Adam. Second Edition. 8vo, price 20s., half-bound.

Ward's Safe Guide to Investment.

A TREATISE on INVESTMENTS; being a Popular Exposition of the Advantages and Disadvantages of each kind of Investment, and of the liability to Depreciation and Loss. By Robert Arthur Ward, Solicitor, Maidenhead, Berkshire. Fourth Edition, with Additions. Price 2s. *(Sd.,* cloth.

Goschen's (the Right Hon. Geo. J., M.P.) Theory of the Foreign Exchanges.

Ninth Edition. One Volume, 8vo, price 6s.

LONDON: EFFINGHAM WILSON, KOYAL EXCHANGE.

Hankey's Principles of Banking.

Its UTILITY and ECONOMY; with Remarks on the Working and Management of the Bank of England. By Thomson Hankey, Esq., M.P., formerly Governor of the Bank of England. 1 volume, 8vo. Third Edition. Price 6s.

Schmidt's Foreign Banking Arbitration:

Its Theory and Practioo. A Handbook of Foreign Exchanges, Bullion, Stocks, and Shares, based upon the New Currencies, &c. By Hermann Schmidt. Price 12.

Wilson's Author's Guide.

A Guide to Authors; showing how to correct the press, according to the mode adopted and understood by Printers. On Sheet. Price *6d.*

Richards's Oliver Cromwell:

An Historical Tragedy, in a Prologue and Four Acts. By Alfred Bate Richards. Dedicated by permission to Thomas Carlyle. Fourth Edition. Price 2.

Rose's Columbus:

An Historical Play, in Five Acts. By Edward Rose. Price 2s.

Adams's Queen Jane:

An Historical Tragedy, in Five Acts. By C. Warren Adams. Price 2s.

Elwes's Through Spain by Rail in 1872.

One vol., 8vo. Price 10s. *6d.*

Elwes's Legend of the Mount; or, the Days of Chivalry.

By Alfred Elwes. With a Frontispiece by Alfred Elwes, Jun. One vol. fcap. 8vo. Price 3s. 6i., cloth.

Twelve True Tales of the Law.

By Copia Fandi, S.C.L., of the Honorable Society of-'s Inn, Bar rister-at-Law. Cheap Edition. Price Is.

Beauvoisin's French Verbs at a Glance.

By Mariot De Beauvoisin. Price Is.

Wilson's Time and Money Tables for Calculating Seamen's Wages. ,

Showing the exact Rateable Time, in calendar months and days, from any one day in the year to another; also, the amount of Wages due for such periods, and at any rating, from 10. up to £50 per annum. Second Edition. Price *10s.,* cloth.

Smith's Legal Forms for Common Use.

Being 250 Precedents, with Introductions and Notes, arranged under the following heads:—1. Negotiable Instruments—2. Securities—3. Receipts and Acknowledgments—*i.* Partnership—5. Master and Servant—6. Landlord and Tenant—7. Arbitrations—8. County Court Forms—9. Conveyances—10. Marriage Settlements—II. Wills—12. Miscellaneous. By James Walter Smith, Esq., LL.D., of the Inner Temple, Barrister-atLaw. Ninth Edition. Price 3. 6rf. , cloth.

Bellairs. on American and Canadian Securities,

An Analysis for the Use of English Investors. Price *5s.,* cloth.

White's Linen and Linen Yarn Trades' Ready Reckoner.

Containing 88,000 calculations. Price 20., cloth.' j

Shaw's Fire Surveys;.

A Summary of the Principles to be observed in estimating the Risks of Building. By Captain Shaw, of the London Fire Brigade. Price 10. *6d.*

Shaw's Records of the late London Fire Engine Establishment.

Price 21.. ',.:

Besemeres' Success in India!

And how to attain it, with the Roads to take and the Paths to avoid. By John Daly Besemekes. Price Is.;

Rickard's Practical Mining.

Fully and familiarly Described. By George Rickard. Price *2s. 6d.,* cloth. I

Barry's Russian Metallurgical Works;

Iron, Copper, and Gold concisely described. Price 5.

§ *m* ——g

I I 10 LONDON: EFFINGHAM WILSON, KOYAL EXCHANGE. i I

Bosanquet's Universal Simple Interest Tables,

Showing the Interest of any sum for any number of days at 100 different rates, from A to 12 per cent. inclusive; also the Interest of any sum for one day at each of the above rates, by single pounds up to one hundred, by hundreds up to forty thousand, and thence by longer intervals up to fifty million pounds—with an additional Table showing the Interest of any number of pounds for one quarter, half-year, or year, at each of the above rates, less income tax from one penny to one shilling in the pound. By Bernard Tindal Bosanquet. 8vo, pp. 480. Price *21s.,* cloth.

Bosanquet's Simple Interest Tables,

For Facilitating the Calculating of Interest at all rates, from one thirtysecond upwards. By Bernard Tindal Bosanquet. Price *5s.,* cloth.

Roney's Rambles on Railways.

With Maps, Diagrams, and Appendices. By Sir Cusack P. Honey, B.A. One Volume, 8vo. Price reduced to *6s.,* cloth.

Michell's Tariff of Customs' Duties LEVIED on the EUROPEAN FRONTIER of the EMPIRE of RUSSIA and KINGDOM of POLAND, from the 1st (13th) of January, 1869. Translated by T. Michell, Her Britannic Majesty's Consul at St. Petersburg, and Revised by the Imperial Russian Department of Trade and Manufactures. 4to. Price 13j. *fid.,* in wrapper. Supplement No. 1, *2s. 6d.*

Long's Popular Guide to matters relating to the Income Tax, the Inhabited House Duty, and the Land Tax.

Third Thousand Revised and Enlarged. By J. P. A. Long, Surveyor of Taxes. Price *Is. 6d.*

Seyd's Bullion and Foreign Exchanges,

Theoretically and Practically Considered; followed by a defence of Double Valuation, with special reference to the proposed system of Universal Coinage. By Ernest Seyd. One Volume, 8vo, pp. 700. Price 20., cloth.

Smith's Odes of Horace, (Books 1 and 2), Rendered into English Verse, with the Latin in parallel pages. By James Walter Smith, Esq., LL.D. Price *5s.,* cloth elegant.

Garratt's Exchange Tables,

To Convert the Moneys of Brazil, the River Plate Ports, Chili, Peru, California, and Lisbon (Milreis and Reis, Dollars and Reals, Dollars and Cents), into British Currency, and vice versa, at all rates of Exchange that can be required, varying by eighths of a penny. By John and Charles Garratt. Price 10s., cloth.

Wilson's Gathered Together: Poems.

By William Wilson, Author of "A Little Earnest Book upon a Great Old Subject; or, Chapters upon Poetry and Poets," "Such is Life: Sketches and Poems," &c. Second Edition, fcap. 8vo, price 5s., cloth.

"Mr. Wilson has added to his acknowledged claims as one of the best poets of the day."—*Hell's Weekly Messenger.* "A fine and lofty spirit pervades these pieces, one and all. They are in every respect worthy of praise."—*Observer.*

"This author has no mean poetic power. The last poem in the book is one of great beauty."—*Literary Gazette.*

"He thinks loftily and feels intensely. "—*Leader.*

"Already favorably known in the literary world. The present volume will not detract from his previous reputation. "—*Morning Post.*

"He aims at originality in his thoughts and his diction, and we may safely say he has succeeded. A collection of the highest merit."—*Court Journal.*

Dunham's Multiplication and Division Tables,

From-ijnd to 10,000,000; adapted to every Calculation. Price 21s.

Dunham's Tables,

Rules and Definitions of Arithmetic, Geometry, Mensuration, aud Trigonometry. Price 2s.

Dunham's Domestic Tables for Pounds and Ounces.

On a Card, price *Is.*

Kaech's Mercantile Tables.

Showing the Cost Value of all principal Staples of Indian Produce on the basis of First Cost, at a certain rate of Freight, but different rates of Exchange, together with a *pro forma* Invoice based on Actual Charges and relating to each Article, by Alex. Kaech.

Newman's Summary of the Law relating to Cheques on Bankers.

Second Edition, price 2s.

'- 1-*m* 12 LONDON: EFFINGHAM WILSON, ROYAL EXCHANGE.,j

Parnell's Land and Houses.

The Investor's Guide to the Purchase of Freehold and Leasehold Ground Rents, Houses, and Land; Observations on the Management of the same, with Tables. Third Edition, price Is.

Pearce's Merchant's Clerk.

A short Exposition of the Laws and Customs regulating the principal operations of the Counting House. Eighth Edition. Price Is.

Ham's Revenue and Mercantile VadeMecum.

An Epitome of the Laws, Regulations, and Practice of Customs, Inland Revenue, and Mercantile Marine. Together with Statistical and other Information. Price *12s. 6d.*

Crosbie and Law's Tables for the Immediate Conversion of Products into Interest, at Twenty-nine Rates, viz.:

From One to Eight per cent. inclu-

sive, proceeding by Quarter Rates, each Rate occupying a single Opening, Hundreds of Products being Represented by Units. By Andrew Crosbie & William C. Law, of Lloyd's Banking Company, Limited; Head Office, Birmingham. Price 10s. *6d.*

Robert's Parliamentary Buff Book.

Being an Analysis of the Divisions of the House of Commons. Session 1875, price 6s. Session 1874, price 6s. Session 1873, price 6s.; Session 1872, price 6s. ; Session 1871, price 5s.; Session 1870, price 5s.; Session 1869, price 4s. Sessions 1866, 1867, 1868, price 5s.

City of London Directory.

Contents: Conveyance Guide, Streets Guide, Alphabetical Directory, Traders' Guide, Public Companies' Directory, Livery Companies' Guide, Corporation Directory. The whole forming a complete Directory to the City of London. Price 10s. 6d., published annually.

Wine:

An Authoritative Defence of its Use. By N. M., a Graduate of Cambridge University and a Clergyman of the Church of England. Price 2.

Besemeres' No Actress; a Stage Doorkeeper's Story.

By John Daly Besemeres. Price 3s. 6d.

Orridge's Account of the Citizens of London

And their Rulers, from 1060 to 1867, and a Calendar of the Mayors and Sheriffs from 1189 to 1867. Price 10s. 6d.

A Table showing the Return on silOO Money Invested in Stock

Bearing Interest at 1 to 10 per cent. on Nominal Capital from 1 to 100. Cloth, Is.

Fairlie's Railways or no Railways.

Narrow Gauge, Economy with Efficiency, *v.* Broad Gauge, Costliness with Extravagance. Illustrated with Photographs, Woodcuts, &c. By Robert F. Fairlie. Price 2s. 6d.

Jones's Time Table and Tables for Calculating Interest at all rates per cent.

Price Is.

Ansell's Royal Mint;

Its Working, Conduct, and Operations, fully and practically explained. Illustrated with Engravings. Third Edition, greatly enlarged, 1 vol. imperial 8vo, price 12s.

Nicholson's Science of Exchanges.

Eourth Edition, revised and enlarged, price 5s.

Cohn's Tables of Exchange

Between England, France, Belgium, Switzerland, and Italy. Converting Francs into Sterling and Sterling into Francs. Cloth, 10s. 6d.

Cohn's Table of Exchanges between Germany and England,

By means of which any amount of Reichstnarcs may be converted into Sterling by Seventy-six Rates of Exchange. Cloth. Price *3s.*

Cohn's Stock Exchange Arbitrageur,

To which is added an Introduction explanatory of the Decimal System, and Tables showing the exact amount of Interest to be added to the calculations, together with a chapter on " OPTIONS." Price 2s. 6d.

Schultz's Universal Dollar Tables,

Epitome of Rates from $4.80 to $4.90 per £, and from 3s. lOd. to 4s. 6d. per $, with an Introductory Chapter on the Coinages and Exchanges of the world. Price 10s. 6d.

I 14 LONDON: EFFINGHAM WILSON, ROYAL EXCHANGE.

Schultz's Universal Interest and General Percentage Tables.

For the use of Bankers, Merchants, and Brokers, in all parts of the world. Applicable to all Calculations of Interest, Discount, Commission, and Brokerage on any given amount, in any Currency, from 1 per cent. to 15 per cent. per annum, by one Quarter per cent. progressively. On the Decimal System. With a Treatise on the Currency of the World, and numerous Examples for Self-instruction. Price 15.

Schultz's Universal Dollar Tables.

Complete United States Edition. Covering all Exchanges between the United States and Great Britain, France, Belgium, Switzerland, Italy, Spain, and Germany.

From $4-50 Cents to $5-50 per Pound Sterling, or from 4 Francs 50 Centimes to 5 Francs 50 Centimes per Dollar, or from 4 Pesetas 50 Cents to 5 Pesetas 50 Cents per Dollar, or from $4-50 to $5

50 per 20 Gold Marcs. For the use of Bankers, Merchants, and Brokers. Price 25$.

Schultz's English-German Exchange Tables,

From 20 Marks to 21 Marks per £, by-025 Marks per £ progressively. Price 5s.

Sternberg's Crisis of 1876:

An Epitome of its Causes and Effects, together with suggestions as to various Remedies. By M. Sternberg. Price 2s.

Young's Royal Exchange Marine Insurance Tables,

For the use of Brokers, Merchants, &c. Cloth, price 2s.

Mercier & Strettell's Manual of American Railroad Securities.

"Gives some very sound and seasonable counsel about the better class of American mortgage bonds."—*Times.*

"Draws an interesting comparison between the position of the preferences of leading English railways as compared with the similar securities of American railways."—*Economist.* "A useful little manual."—*Railway News.*
Second Edition. Price Is. 6d.

Mercier & Strettell's Manual of Foreign Railwav Securities.

Contents.—1. Russian Railway Shares. 2. French Railway Shares and Obligations. 3. Italian and Spanish Railway Obligations. 4. Miscellaneous. 5. The Suez Canal Company. Price 2s. 6d.
MISCELLANEOUS LIST. VALUABLE WORKS OF REFERENCE, COMMERCIAL, LEGAL, GEOGRAPHICAL, AXD STATISTICAL.

Ager's Telegram Code,

For the use of Bankers, Merchants, and Shipowners. Price 42s.

Adlington's Anglo-French Produce Tables,

Transferring the Cost of any Article from Sterling per Cwt. into Francs or Lires (Italian) per 100 Kilogrammes, at Exchanges ranging from to 32. Price *2s. 6d.*

Arnould's Marine Insurance.

A Treatise on the Law of Marine Insurance and Average; with References to the American Cases and the later Continental Authorities. By Sir Joseph

Abnculd (Puisne Judge, Bombay).

Fourth Edition, in 2 vols., royal 8vo. Price £2 12. *6d.,* cloth.

Anderson's Practical Mercantile Correspondence.

A Collection of Modern Letters of Business, containing a Dictionary of Commercial Technicalities. Twenty-first Edition, revised and enlarged. By William Anderson. Price 5s.

Byles' Law of Bills of Exchange, Promissory Notes, Bank Notes, and Cheques.

By the Right Hon. Sir John Bernard Byles. Eleventh Edition.
Price *25s.*

Bagehots' Lombard Street.

A description of the Money Market. Sixth Edition. Price *7s.* 6t?.

Bank of England (The), Minimum Rates of Discount during the Past Thirty-two Years, and the Average Rate of each Year.

Price *Is.* Published Annually.
g—

I I 16. LONDON: EFFINGHAM WILSON, BOYAL EXCHANGE.

Banking Almanack (The), Directory, Year-

Book, and Diarv.

A Parliamentary and complete Banking Directory, Published Annually.
Price 7s. 6d.

Blackstone's (Sir W.) Commentaries on the Laws of England.

By Chittt.

Twenty-first Edition. By Hargrave, Sweet, Couch, and Welsby. 4 vols., 8vo. Price £1 5.

Bradshaw's Railway Shareholders' Manual.

Published Annually. Price *lis.,* cloth.

Brande's Dictionary of Science, Literature and Art;

Comprising the History, Description, and Scientific Principles of every Branch of Human Knowledge; with the Derivation and Definition of all the Terms in General Use. Edited by W. T. Brande, F.R.S.L. and E., and Rev. Geo. W. Cox, M.A.

New Edition, revised and corrected; including a Supplement, and numerous Wood Engravings. 3 vols. 8vo, cloth. Price £3 3.

Brooke's Treatise ori the Office and Practice of a Notary in England,

Fourth Edition. With Alterations and Additions. In 8vo, boards. Price 21.

Carter's Practical Book-Keeping,

Adapted to Commercial and Judicial Accounting, with sets of books and forms of Accounts for' different professions and trades. Third Edition. Revised and Enlarged. Price 7. *6d.*

Chitty on Bills of Exchange and Promissory Notes.

A Treatise on Bills of Exchange, Promissory Notes, Cheques on Bankers, Bankers' Cash Notes, and Bank Notes; with References to the Law of Scotland, France, and America. By John A. Russell, LL.B., and David Maclachlan, M. A., Barristers-at-Law.

Tenth Edition, in royal 8vo, cloth. Price £1 8s.

Crump's Theory of Stock Exchange Speculation.

Fourth Edition. Price 10s. 6i.

M -W

Crump's Practical Treatise on Banking, Currency, and the Exchanges.

By Abtutjh Chump, Bank Manager. Price 6s.

Egyptian Commercial Calculating Tables.

Price 12s.

Every Man's Own Lawyer.

A Handy book of the Principles of Law and Equity, comprising the Rights and Wrongs of Individuals, Landlord and Tenant, Sales, Purchases, Master and Servant, Workmen and Apprentices, Elections and Registrations, Libel and Slander, Mercantile and Commercial Laws, Contracts and Agreements, Railways and Carriers, Companies and Associations, Partners and Agents, Bankruptcy and Debtors, Trade Marks and Patents, Husband and Wife, Dower and Divorce, Executor and Trustees, Heirs, Devisees, and Legatees, Poor Men's Law Suits, Game and Fishery Laws, Parish and Criminal Law, Forms of Wills, Agreements, Bonds, Notices, &c. &c. By a Baebistee. Thirteenth Edition. Price 6s. 8d.

Fortunate Men: how they made Money and Won Renown.

Price 3s. *Gd.*

Financial Register (The) and Stock Exchange Manual,

Showing Capital, Dividends, and Prices of the Public Funds,

Colonial and Foreign Debts, of Banking, Finance, Insurance, Mining, Railway, Shipping, Telegraph, Water, and Gas, and other British and

Foreign Joint Stock Companies. Published Annually. Price 25s.

Gilbart's Principles and Practice of Banking.

Thoroughly revised and adapted to the Practice of the present day. Price 16s.

Goodfellow's Merchants' and Shipmasters'

Ready Calculator.

Exhibiting at one View *the solid contents* of all kinds of Packages and Casks. By J. Goodpellow. Price *Is. Gd.*

Harben's Weight Calculator.

From 1 lb. to 15 Tons, at 300 Progressive Rates, from 1 penny to 168 shillings per Hundredweight. Second Edition. Price 30s.

Hardwick's Trader's Check Book

For Buying and Selling by the Hundredweight, Ton, or by Measure, &c. Price 2s. 6d.

Holdsworth's Law of Landlord and Tenant. Price Is.

18 LONDON: EFFINGHAM WILSON, KOYAL EXCHANGE.

Holdsworth's Law of Wills and Executors. Price Is.

Holdsworth's Law of the County Court.

Price Is.

Hopkins' (Manley) Handbook of Average.

Third Edition, 1 vol., 8to. Price 18s.

Hopkins' (Manley) A Manual of Marine Assurance.

One vol., 8vo. Price 18.

Hoppus's Tables

For Measuring the Solid Contents of Timber, Stone, &c. Price 3s. *Sd.*

Houghton's Mercantile Tables

For Ascertaining the Value of Goods, Bought or Sold by the Hundredweight, at any price from one farthing to twenty pounds per Hundredweight; or by the Ton, one shilling to four hundred pounds per Ton.

Price £1 Is.

Inwood's Tables

For the Purchasing of Estates, Freehold, Copyhold, or Leasehold Annuities, Advowsons, &c, and for the Renewing of Leases held under Cathedral Churches, Colleges, or other Corporate Bodies, for Terms of Years; also for Valuing Reversionary Estates, &c.

Nineteenth Edition. 12mo, boards. Price 8s.

Jevons's Money and the Mechanism of Exchange.

Price 5s.

Johnston's New Dictionary of Geography,

Descriptive, Physical, Statistical, and Historical: forming a complete General Gazetteer of the World. By Alexandeb Keith Johnston, F.R.S.E., F.R.G.S., F. G.S. j Geographer at Edinburgh in Ordinary to Her Majesty. In One Volume of 1440 pages; comprising nearly 50,000 Names of Places. 8vo, oloth, price £110s.; or strongly half-bound in russia, with flexible backs, £115s.

King's Interest Tables,

Calculated at 5 per cent., exhibiting at one glance the interest of any sum, from one pound to three hundred and sixty-five pounds; and (advancing by hundreds) to one thousand pounds; and (by thousands) to ten thousand pounds; from one day to three hundred and sixty-five days. Also, Monthly Interest Tables, Yearly Interest Tables, and Commission Tables. Price 7s. 6(Z.

J Lawson's History of Banking.

Second Edition. One Volume, 8vo. (Scarce.)

Lax ton's Builders' Price Book,

Containing upwards of 72,000 Prices, carefully corrected and revised according to the present prices of materials and labour. Published Annually. Price 4s.

Laurie's High-Rate Tables of Simple Interest,

At 5, 6, 7, 8, 9 and J per cent. per annum, from 1 day to 100 days, 1 month to 12 months. Also copious Tables of Commission or Brokerage, from one eighth to ten per cent. By James Laurie. Price 7s.

Lee's Laws of Shipping and Insurance.

Ninth Edition. One Volume. Price 12s. *6d.*

Levi's Commercial Law.

The Commercial Law of the World, or the Mercantile Law of the United Kingdom, compared with the Codes and Laws of Commerce of Foreign Countries. By Leone Levi, Esq.

Two vols., 8vo. Price 35s.

London Banks, Credit, Discount, and Finance Companies.

Their Directors, Managers, Capital and Keserve Funds and Dividends. Published twice a year. Price 2s. *6d.*

Louis's Anglo-French Calculator.

A Beady Reckoner for facilitating Trade with France. Price Is.

Macleod's Elements of Banking.

Price 7s. *M.*

Martin's History of Lloyd's and Marine Insurance in Great Britain.

Price 14s.

M'Culloch's Dictionary, Practical, Theoretical, and Historical, of Commerce and Commercial Navigation.

Illustrated with Maps and Plans. By J. B. M'culloch, Esq. New Edition, corrected, enlarged, and improved: including a New Supplement. 8vo, cloth, price £3 3s.; or £3 10s., half-bound in russia, with flexible back.

m= = m j 20 LONDON: EFFINGHAM WILSON, ROYAL EXCHANGE.

M'Culloch's Dictionary, Geographical, Statistical, and Historical,

Of the various Countries, Places, and Principal Natural Objects, in the World. By J. R. M'culloch, Esq. Illustrated with Six large Maps.

New Edition, with a Supplement, comprising the Population of Great Britain from the Census of 1851. 2 vols., 8vo, cloth. Price £4 4s.

McArthur's Policy of Marine Insurance Popularly Explained.

With a Chapter on Occasional Clauses. Second Edition. Price 3s. *6d.*

Martin's Statesman's Year Book;

A Statistical and Historical Annual of the States of the Civilised World for Politicians and Merchants. Revised after Official Returns. Price 10s. 6c?. Published Annually.

Merchant Shippers (Export) of London, Birmingham, Wolverhampton, and Walsall,

With their respective Trading Ports and the Class of Goods they customarily ship. Alphabetically arranged. Price 12s.

Nicholson's Science of Exchanges.

Fourth Edition. Revised and Enlarged. Price 5s.

Purdy's City Life: its Trade and Finance.

Price 7s. *6d.*

Price's (Bonamy) Currency and Banking.

Price 6s.

Poor's Manual of the Railroads of the United States,

Showing their Mileage, Stocks, Bonds, Cost, Traffic, Earnings, Expenses, and Organizations, with a Sketch of their Rise, Progress, Influence, &c. Together with an Appendix, containing a full Analysis of the Debts of the United States and of the several States, published Annually. Price 24s.

Ranee's Tables of Compound Interest,

Eor every *i* per cent. from *i* to 10 per cent., and for every year from 1 to 100. Price 21s.

Stonehouse's Profit Table for Investments,

Showing the actual profit per cent. per annum to be derived from any Purchase or Investment. Price Is. *%d.*

Shelton's Tables for Ascertaining the English Prices of French Goods.

To which is added a Revised Scale of French and English Measures. Price 2. 6rf.

Simmonds's Dictionary of Trade Products,

Commercial and Manufacturing; with the Moneys, Weights, and Measures of all Nations. Price *7s. 6d.,* half-bound.

Skinner's Stock Exchange Year-Book and Diary,

Containing a Digest of Information relating to the Joint Stock Companies and Public Securities known to the Markets of the United Kingdom. Published Annually. Price 5s.

Smith's (Adam) Wealth of Nations.

Edited by M'culloch. 1 vol., 8vo. Price 16s.

Smith's Compendium of Mercantile Law.

One Volume. Royal 8vo. Price £1 16s.

St. Leonard's (Lord) Handy Book on Property Law.

. In a Series of Letters. 12mo, cloth. Seventh Edition. Price 5s.

Stevens on the Stowage of Ships and their Cargoes:

With information regarding Freights, Charter-parties, &c. Sixth Edition, price 21.

Schonberg's Chain Rule.

A Manual of Brief Commercial Arithmetic: being an easy, simple, and efficient auxiliary in the working of difficult and complicated problems. Price *Is.*

Telegraph Code (International),

Compiled for the use of Bankers, Merchants, Manufacturers, Contractors, Brokers, and Sharebrokers, for the Economical and Secret Transmission of Mercantile Telegrams. Price 25s.

Ure's Dictionary of Arts, Manufactures, and Mines.

Containing a clear Exposition of their Principles and Practice. By Andrew Uke, F.R.S., M.G.S., M.A.S. Lond.; M. Acad. N.L. Philad.; S. Ph. Soc. N. Germ. Hanov.; Mulii, &c. &c. Edited by Robert Hunt, F.R.S.

New Edition, corrected. 3 vols., Svo, with nearly 2000 Engravings on j Wood. Price £5 5s., cloth.

11 22 LONDON: EFFINGHAM WILSON, ROYAL EXCHANGE. I

Williams and Lafont's French and English Commercial Correspondence.

A Collection of Modern Mercantile Letters in French and English, with. their Translations on opposite pages. Second Edition. Price 4. *6d.*

Wade's Cabinet Lawyer.

A Popular Digest of the Laws of England, with the Criminal Law of England and a Dictionary of Law Terms, &c.

A New Edition. Fcap. 8yo. Price *10s.* 6i., cloth.

Warren's Blackstone.

Blackstone's Commentaries, systematically Abridged and adapted to the existing state of the Law and Constitution, with great Additions. By Samuel Warren, Esq., Q.C. 1850.

Second Edition, in post 8vo, cloth. Price 18.

Wordsworth's Law of Banking, Mining, and General Joint-Stock Companies Not requiring express authority of Parliament. By C. Wordsworth. Sixth Edition. Price 15s.

BLACK'S TOURIST'S GUIDES. *s. d.*

Scotland s 6

England 10 6

English Lakes 50

Wales.. 50

Ireland 50

Where shall we go?

A Guide to the Watering Places of the British Islands..30

Channel Islands, Jersey, Guernsey, Alderney 3 c

Dorset, Devon, and Cornwall....50

Isle of Wight.10

London and Environs....86 *These Ouides are profusely Illustrated, and contain excellent Maps.* BADEKER'S CONTINENTAL GUIDE BOOKS.

Belgium and Holland.

The Rhine from Rotterdam to Constance.

With 15 Maps and 16 Plans, 5s.

With 11 Maps and 16 Plans, 8s.

Switzerland.

With 21 Maps, 7 Plans, and 7 Panoramas, 6j.

Paris and its Environs.

With 2 Maps and 19 Plans, 5s.

Northern Italy and Corsica.

With 6 Maps and 16 Plans, 6s.

Central Italy and Rome.

With 3 Maps and 8 Plans, 6s.

Southern Italy, Sicily, Malta, Lipari Islands, Carthage, and Athens.

Traveller's Manual of Conversation, English, French, German, and Italian, 3s.

With 3 Maps and 14 Plans, 5s.

Northern Germany.

With 11 Maps and 27 Plans, 5s.

South Germany and Austria.

With 6 Maps and 7 Plans, 6s.

ff24 LONDON: EFFINGHAM WILSON, ROYAL EXCHANGE. I MURRAY'S FOR-

EIGN & ENGLISH HANDBOOKS.

I. THE CONTINENT, &c. HANDBOOK—TRAVEL TALK, in English, French, German, and Italian, adapted for Englishmen Abroad, or Foreigners in England. 18mo, 3. *Gd.* HANDBOOK—HOLLAND, Belgium, and the Rhine, to Mayence. Post 8vo, 6. HANDBOOK—NORTH GERMANY and the Rhine to Switzerland. Map. Post 8vo, 6.

HANDBOOK—SOUTH GERMANY, The Tyrol, Bavaria, Austria, Salzburg, Styria, Hungary, and the Danube from Ulm to the Black Sea. Map. Post 8vo, 10. HANDBOOK—SWITZERLAND, The Alps of Savoy and Piedmont. Maps. Post 8vo, *9s.* HANDBOOK—FRANCE, Normandy, Brittany, The French Alps, Dauphine, Provence, and the Pyrenees. Maps. 2 vols. Post 8vo, 12. HANDBOOK—SPAIN, Andalusia, Grenada, Madrid, &c. With Supplement, containing Inns and Railways, &c, 1861. Maps. 2 vols. Post 8vo, 24s. HANDBOOK—PORTUGAL, Lisbon, &c. Map. Post 8vo, 9. HANDBOOK—NORTH ITALY, Piedmont, Nice, Lombardy, Venice, Parma, Modena, and Romagna. Maps. Post 8vo, 10. HANDBOOK—CENTRAL ITALY, Lucca, Tuscany, Florence, Umbria, The Marches, and the Patrimony of St. Peter. Map. Post 8vo, 10. HANDBOOK—ROME AND ITS ENVIRONS. Map. Post 8vo, 10. HANDBOOK—SOUTH ITALY, Two Sicilies, Naples, Pompeii, Herculaneum, Vesuvius, Abruzzi, &c. Maps. Post 8vo, 10. HANDBOOK—SICILY, Palermo, Messina, Catania, Syracuse, &c. Plans. Post 8vo, 12. HANDBOOK—CORSICA AND SARDINIA. Maps. Post 8vo, 4. HANDBOOK—EGYPT, The Nile, Alexandria, Cairo, Thebes, and the Overland Route to India. Map. Post 8vo, 15. HANDBOOK—GREECE, The Ionian Islands, Athens, Albania, Thessaly, and Macedonia. Maps. Post 8vo, 15. HANDBOOK—TURKEY, Constantinople, and Asia Minor. Maps. Post 8vo, 15. HANDBOOK—DENMARK, Norway, Sweden, and Iceland. Maps. Post 8vo, 15. HANDBOOK—RUSSIA, St. Peters-

burg, Moscow, Finland, &c. Maps. Post 8vo, 15. HANDBOOK—INDIA, Bombay, and Madras. Map. 2 vols. Post 8vo, 24. HANDBOOK—HOLY LAND, Syria, Palestine, Sinai, Edom, and the Syrian Desert. Maps. 2 vols. Post 8vo, 24. HANDBOOK—PARIS AND ITS ENVIRONS. Map. Post 8vo, 3. *Gd.*

II. ENGLAND.

HANDBOOK—MODERN LONDON. Map. 16rao, 3. *Gd.* HANDBOOK—KENT AND SUSSEX. Map. Post 8vo, 10. HANDBOOK—SURREY, HANTS, AND THE ISLE OF WIGHT. Map. Post 8vo,10. HANDBOOK—BERKS, BUCKS, AND OXFORDSHIRE. Map. Post 8vo, 7. *Gd.* HANDBOOK—WILTS, DORSET, AND SOMERSET. Map. Post 8vo, 10. HANDBOOK—DEVON AND CORNWALL. Map. Post 8vo, 12. HANDBOOK—NORTH AND SOUTH WALES. Maps. 2 vols. 7. each. HANDBOOK—GLOUCESTER, HEREFORD, & WORCESTER. Map. Post8vo,9s. HANDBOOK—SHROPSHIRE AND CHESHIRE. Map. Post 8vo, 10. HANDBOOK—EASTERN COUNTIES: Essex, Cambridge, Suffolk and Norfolk. Maps. Post 8vo, 12. HANDBOOK—DERBY, NOTTS, LEICESTER, AND STAFFORD. Map. Post 8vo, 7. *Gd.* HANDBOOK—YORKSHIRE. Map and Plans. Post 8vo, 12.

HANDBOOK—DURHAM AND NORTHUMBERLAND. Map, 9.

HANDBOOK—WESTMORELAND AND CUMBERLAND. Map. Post 8vo, 6.

HANDBOOK—SCOTLAND. Maps and Plans. Post 8vo, 9.

HANDBOOK—IRELAND. Map. Post 8vo, 12s.

HANDBOOK—SOUTHERN CATHEDRALS. —200 Illustrations. 2 vols., 24.

HANDBOOK—EASTERN CATHEDRALS. 18.

HANDBOOK—WESTERN CATHEDRALS. 16.

HANDBOOK—NORTHERN CATHEDRALS. 2 vols., 21.

LONDON: EFFINGHAM WILSON, BOYAL EXCHANGE.

CPSIA information can be obtained
at www.ICGtesting.com
Printed in the USA
BVOW03s1948020317
477625BV00007B/105/P

9 781236 562197